You Can Soar Like an Eagle

"I can enthusiastically recommend *You Can Soar Like an Eagle.* The book is very warm and encouraging and is filled with illustrations of people from all walks of life who have learned to soar, whatever their circumstance. . . . Nell Mohney's faith in God and in the human spirit is an inspiration for all."

—Richard C. Looney, retired United Methodist Bishop,
President of The Foundation for Evangelism,
Lake Junaluska, North Carolina

"What Nell Mohney does in this uplifting book is the same thing she does at her popular seminars all over the country. She tells stories about ordinary people who surmount devastating problems by relying on faith, using her unique voice to inspire readers that they are not alone and that God cares for them."

—Karin Glendenning, Book Editor,
Chattanooga Free Press

"*You Can Soar Like an Eagle* gently carries you through the winds and turbulence that life inevitably brings to us all, and it offers an incredible picture from the life of the eagle that is impossible to miss. Once you are introduced to the strength, wisdom, and command of this great bird's way of life, you will be inspired to embrace it for your own. . . . Compelling and memorable!"

—Jan Silvious,
Christian counselor, speaker, author

Nell W. Mohney

You Can Soar Like an Eagle

DIMENSIONS
FOR LIVING
NASHVILLE

YOU CAN SOAR LIKE AN EAGLE

Copyright © 2004 by Dimensions for Living

This book is printed on acid-free, elemental-chlorine–free paper.

Library of Congress Cataloging-in-Publication Data

Mohney, Nell.
   You can soar like an eagle / Nell W. Mohney.
     p. cm.
   ISBN 0-687-04469-3 (pbk.)
   1. Christian life—Methodist authors. I. Title.

   BV4501.3.M645 2004
   248.4—dc22

2003023404

Scripture quotations noted KJV are from the King James Version of the Bible.

Scripture quotations noted NIV are taken from the HOLY BIBLE: NEW INTER-NATIONAL VERSION®. Copyright © 1973, 1978, 1984 by the International Bible Society. Used by permission of Zondervan Bible Publishers.

Scripture quotations marked NKJV are taken from the New King James Version. Copyright © 1979, 1980, 1982 by Thomas Nelson Inc., Publishers.

Scripture quotations noted NRSV are from the New Revised Standard Version of the Bible, copyright © 1989, by the Division of Christian Education of the National Council of the Churches of Christ in the United States of America. Used by permission.

Scripture quotations noted TLB are from The Living Bible, copyright © 1971 by Tyndale House Publishers, Wheaton, IL 60189. Used by permission. All rights reserved.

Lyrics on page 114 are from "On Eagle's Wings." Copyright © 1979, OCP Publications, 5536 NE Hassalo, Portland, OR 97213. All rights reserved. Used with permission.

04 05 06 07 08 09 10 11 12 13—10 9 8 7 6 5 4 3 2 1
MANUFACTURED IN THE UNITED STATES OF AMERICA

To Dr. Robert H. Schuller, who through his books, television ministry, and personal example has strengthened my faith in Jesus Christ, thus enabling me to believe that I, too, may soar like an eagle over life's vicissitudes.

Contents

Foreword

*Y*ou Can Soar Like an Eagle is an incredible book created by Dr. Nell Mohney. She packs an amazing amount of inspiration, energy, and encouragement in an easy-to-read book that will inspire you to soar above the storms and difficulties of life. More than a practical guide though, this book shows us how faith in God's unwavering love can lift us up on eagles' wings. She teaches us how to find the energy, creativity, and passion that exists inside each of us so we might be empowered to learn how to escape the bog and mire of our lives and launch a new life on the proud wings of victory.

After reading Nell Mohney's marvelous book, I was inspired to implement the strategies in my own life and to share her story with everyone I know. As you can tell, I'm excited about *You Can Soar Like an Eagle*. I think this is a marvelous book. But it is not just a how-to book; it is a beautiful love story that teaches us how faith in God's unwavering love can help our spirits soar. Nell Mohney will teach you to use your faith to overcome the negative forces that tend to hold you back and will empower you to create a more fulfilling life by changing the way you think.

Nell Mohney, a longtime colleague and dear friend, has written the story that she frequently shares with audiences throughout our nation. Few leave a seminar or meeting with her without finding that they have come to see their own tasks and lives in a newer and brighter light. Her winning spirit helped her triumph over tragedy and loss in her own life and gave her wings to soar like the eagles. From her practical ways to seek renewal to her eye-opening dialogue about salvation, she will teach you with clarity and focus how to see the whole picture with eagle eyes.

Besides her work as a nationally known author, Nell Mohney has made a difference in the lives of thousands of people who applaud her presentations. I marvel at her energy and at the influence that she has with audiences all over the country. People across all denominational and cultural barriers love her seminars. She keeps her large audiences of civic or corporate groups spellbound. Men and women, young and old, love her compassion, her enthusiasm, her self-effacing humor, her openness for adventure, and her deep abiding faith. She is known by those who have grown to love her as Cheerful Nell.

You Can Soar Like an Eagle will bring revolutionary change to any person who wants to achieve exciting improvement in his or her personal life. I promise it will be one of the most rewarding and uplifting books you have ever read. It will enrich your life and make your spirit soar.

June Scobee Rodgers

Introduction

But those who hope in the LORD will renew their strength. They will soar on wings like eagles; they will run and not grow weary, they will walk and not be faint. (Isaiah 40:31 NIV)

The eagle, our national bird, is a majestic bird, representing inspiration and courage. According to my research, it is the only bird that will not try to avoid a storm. Though eagles don't seek out storms, when one occurs, they hang on until they can soar above it.

It occurs to me that some people are like eagles. It isn't that these "eagle people" have no storms or difficulties in their lives. All of us do. Storms are a part of the very fabric of life. If you haven't had any storms recently, just wait a little while! What makes them "eagle people" is their tenacious hold on hope. They truly believe what Jesus told us: "In the world [you] shall have tribulation: but be of good cheer; I have overcome the world" (John 16:33 KJV).

When I was growing up, we had a cook named Willie Mae. She was a wonderful person as well as an excellent cook, and every member of my family loved her. She had one major difficulty: worry. She worried about everything. I remember my mother saying to her once, "Willie Mae, you shouldn't worry so much. You should trust the Lord more." Through the years we have laughed often about her reply: "Miz Webb, the Lord said that we would have tribulation in our lives. When it comes, I think he expects me to 'tribulate.'" And "tribulate" she did!

The "eagle people" I know have had plenty of storms in their lives, many of them severe; but instead of worrying, they have drawn upon the inner resources that come from faith to rise above the storms and soar. They have lived with courage and hope, inspiring all around them.

In this book, we will explore the resources available to us as Christians when storms suddenly appear upon our horizons. Among these resources are the Bible, the revealed Word of God; prayer; worship; and the example and encouragement of Christian friends, family members, coworkers, and neighbors. When we use these God-given resources, we can "soar like an eagle"!

Each chapter begins with a key scripture verse. If you have time, you might find it helpful to take a few minutes to read the surrounding biblical text on your own. Likewise, each chapter ends with questions for reflection or discussion to help individuals or groups "dig a little deeper." Some chapters also include "An Eagle Challenge," in which I make specific suggestions for implementing a particular principle in your life. As you read and use the material provided in this book, it is my hope that, like the eagle, you may be a symbol of courage and inspiration to those whose lives you touch.

1

The Mechanics of Soaring

But those who hope in the LORD will renew their strength. They will soar on wings like eagles; they will run and not grow weary, they will walk and not be faint. (Isaiah 40:31 NIV)

Several years ago, we were traveling with friends in the American West when I saw an eagle "mount up" to fly. It was at Yellowstone National Park that the magnificent bird, perched on a rock ledge, opened his seven-foot wingspan to lift off. He didn't take off gradually and diagonally like an airplane, but he "mounted up" like a helicopter.

Later I learned that eagles can soar without flapping their wings. On each of their wings are twelve hundred feathers. At the end of each feather is a fingerlike attachment that opens at lift off, thus enabling the huge bird to catch the wind and soar.

Like the eagle, we Christians are equipped to mount up effortlessly and soar. Though we don't have wings, we do have our own special equipment that helps us tap into the power of God, "mount up," and soar. According to the psalmist, we are "fearfully and wonderfully made" (Psalm 139:14 NIV). Let's consider how some of our natural equipment—specifically, our eyes, our ears, and our brains—provide the mechanics for allowing us either to soar or to fall into defeat.

Our Eyes Help Us Look for God

God has given us eyes more powerful than any Nikon, Minolta, or Canon camera. Our eyes take pictures in living, authentic color; we store these pictures in our minds; and we can see these pictures even years later in our mind's eye. Eagles have a unique ability to look directly into the sun because of two sets of eyelashes, one of which lowers and becomes like sunglasses when facing the sun. Though we don't have that natural ability, we do have the choice to look up for the guidance of God rather than focus on the chaos of daily living. When we choose to focus on God, we seem to have a set of inner eyes. We perceive a new dimension of understanding. These are the eyes we use when we have an "aha!" moment.

Once when I was a young pastor's wife, a girl, Lucy, from our youth group started coming by the parsonage often to talk. She talked about superficial things that were bothering her, but I had the feeling that she was trying to tell me something much deeper. Though I thought of her often and wondered what she wanted to say, I couldn't find the answer.

Then in a quiet time as I prayed, I saw it clearly. Though she didn't have the courage to voice her concerns, she was really saying, "Look, Mrs. Mohney, I'm eighteen years old; I am smart and not unattractive, but I've never had a date. Why?" It was an "aha!" moment.

Since I was working with our young people to plan a Valentine banquet, I knew that two of the most popular boys hadn't yet chosen dates for the event. Though it took a bit of persuasion, I talked the president into inviting Lucy as his date. Then the vice president agreed to call her the next week to go to a movie. It worked like a charm! When those "cool dudes" were seen with Lucy, other boys began to call her. She was launched! It was such fun to watch. God gave me a set of inner eyes to see into the heart of a young girl.

The psalmist expressed his choice to look up for God when he wrote these words: "I will lift up mine eyes unto the hills, from whence cometh my help. My help cometh from the LORD, which made heaven and earth" (Psalm 121:1-2 KJV). These verses remind me of two experiences that demonstrated how choosing to "lift up our eyes" calms the spirit and enables us to see God.

Recently I served as keynote speaker in a large conference for women. Though the audience was wonderful, every minute of the two-and-a-half-day conference was tightly scheduled. At breakfast on the final morning, several women gathered around me, asking questions and inviting me to sign their books. I was beginning to feel overwhelmed by the noise and the pressure—almost claustrophobic. As quickly and as caringly as I could, I excused myself, left the table, and headed for a bench in the rose garden of the lovely conference center. As I breathed slowly and deeply, I lifted my eyes toward the spectacular foliage of the trees on the mountain ahead of me. Not only was I aware of God's beautiful creation all around me, but, in the stillness, I also became aware that my inner eyes seemed to be opened to the very presence of God.

As I stilled my heart amid the beauty of God's creation, I saw in my mind's eye a time of frustration in early parenthood when I was becoming a person I didn't want to be—impatient, irritable, and unhappy. That day, as I knelt beside an unmade bed with my colicky baby crying in an adjacent room, I said sincerely, "Lord, if you can do anything with this warped personality of mine, you can have it as long as I live."

Now, God was reminding me of my promise and asking, "Did

you really mean it?" Nodding, I replied in my heart, "I did." It was as if God enabled me to "get the picture." I realized that God was calling a calmer me to return to those women, many of whom had deep hurts, and be his representative. I suddenly saw that my purpose for being there was not to make me comfortable or successful as a speaker. Because my inner eyes had been opened, I realized that I simply was to help people in the name of Christ.

> *We use our inner eyes when we have an "aha!" moment.*

In addition to helping us see God, our inner, or spiritual, eyes allow us to see other persons—not as they appear, but as God sees them. A number of years ago, I was flying to Richmond, Virginia, to speak. My seatmate looked as if he might be the CEO of a large corporation. He was tall, lean, and tanned. He also was the most negative man I had ever encountered. He was down on the national, state, and county governments and was going to Washington, D.C. to meet with a lobbyist group because Congress was not following his strong suggestions. He talked on and on and then asked, "Where are you going?"

"To Richmond," I replied.

"Why?"

"To speak."

"Where?"

"In a church," I replied. As quick as a flash, he said, "I don't believe in all that spiritual stuff." Everything in me wanted to say, "Well, if you did, maybe you wouldn't be so negative." Instead, I said, "You look like an intelligent man. You must have some reason for that."

In a few moments, the man looked at me and asked, "Do you believe in all that spiritual stuff?"

"With all of my heart, I believe in the Christian faith," I replied sincerely.

He turned and looked at me as if to decide whether or not to trust me. Then he blurted out, "My son is on drugs, and it is tearing my heart out." Suddenly my inner eyes saw a different man. He was no longer a negative complainer who was down on the government. Instead, he was a brokenhearted father who felt helpless in the face of his son's drug addiction.

I let him pour out the whole story, and then I told him what my faith in Christ had meant to me when our twenty-year-old son died following an accident. I also gave him the name of a CEO in my city whose son was two years beyond a successful rehab program. The rest of the story is too long to tell, but it is exciting. The bottom line is that, since our meeting that day, the man's son has become a productive, drug-free member of society; and the entire family is active in a Christian church. How often I have thanked God for inner eyes that revealed the heart of a troubled father and allowed me to be used to begin a process of eternal change in this man's life and family.

That day it occurred to me that in the busy-ness of our fast-paced world, we see only surface situations. I had seen the CEO as a negative, unhappy man with whom I didn't want to waste time. It was only when I had asked myself, "How does God see this man?" that my inner eyes were opened to his real needs. That was what had enabled my spirit to soar like an eagle.

Our Ears Help Us Listen for God

Though our ears may not be as sensitive as those of some of God's other creatures, God has given us an amazing ability to hear, especially if we're listening for a particular sound. When my own children were babies, I could hear their slightest whimper even when they were upstairs in bed and I was downstairs in a room full of people. Even when I was sleeping soundly during the night, I would awaken at their very first cry.

Once I heard the story of a Native American, Tal, who was visiting his friend Tim in New York City. As they walked down Fifth Avenue, Tal suddenly stopped and turned to his friend, saying, "I hear a cricket." Tim laughed uproariously. "You can't possibly hear a cricket in all this traffic, and certainly not on Fifth Avenue."

After looking up and down the street, Tal spotted a fruit vendor; and there on his cart was a cricket. Tim was stunned. "How did you hear that?" he asked his guest. Without answering, Tal took a silver dollar from his pocket and dropped it. Immediately at least a dozen persons stopped to listen. "You see," replied Tal, "we hear what we listen for."

God, through the psalmist, tells us to "be still, and know that I am God" (Psalm 46:10 KJV). If we are to mount up and soar, we must learn to be quiet, listen, and wait upon God. Though we can hear with our inner or spiritual ears in almost any situation, I like to have some sacred spaces in which, upon entering, I can instantly feel God's presence. The sanctuary, chapel, and prayer chapel of my church are such places for me. When I am teaching Sunday school, I like to go early and slip into the prayer chapel to experience God's presence through silence. It is incredible how often a pertinent thought or illustration for the lesson will surface. Often these last-minute insights speak to class members more forcibly than the carefully planned lesson.

I also have a favorite "sacred space" in our home. Actually, it is only a beige-colored recliner in the master bedroom. Most of the time, it is a very secular space. The chair is adjacent to my desk where I do most of my writing. It is even a place where I sometimes watch a TV news program or movie. Yet, when I get into the chair, close the door, and close my eyes in order to "center down" and focus on God, it becomes a very sacred space in which I meet God, read Scripture, meditate, think, and pray. A sacred space, I have learned, has a great deal to do with one's mind-set and attitude. By closing my eyes and changing my thoughts, that beige recliner becomes a sanctuary.

> **Jesus was not agitated or harried, but was calmly confident and supremely sure of his mission.**

When we read the Gospels, we see that Jesus was not agitated or harried, but was calmly confident and supremely sure of his mission. Even in the horrific days of his trial and crucifixion, he moved with serene steadfastness toward the cross. I believe that there is no way Jesus could have lived with such serenity without the regular practice of "going apart" for silence, prayer, and listening for God's direction. Luke 6:12 tells us that before choosing the twelve apostles, Jesus "went out to the mountain to pray; and he spent the night in prayer to God" (NRSV). There are many other examples in the Bible of Jesus going apart for prayer, such as after walking on the water (Matthew 14:23), after healing Peter's mother (Mark 1:35), after feeding the five thousand (Luke 9:18), at the Transfiguration (Luke 9:28), and, of course, in the Garden of Gethsemane (Matthew 26:36).

Abraham of the Old Testament must have practiced quietness on the plains of the Ur of Chaldees. Otherwise, how could God, unknown to Abraham at the time, have communicated with this one who was to be the head of a great nation? After all, Ur was a bristling, metropolitan city—the center of power in the ancient world. The most prosperous citizens were idol makers, and the deity of the city was the moon goddess, Nana. Abraham's father, Terah, was one of the leading idol makers. I don't believe Abraham could have known the true God unless he had learned to still his heart.

Much later, around 700 B.C., the prophet Isaiah wrote, "In quietness and in trust shall be your strength" (Isaiah 30:15 NRSV). The miracle is that Abraham not only heard God speak and was strengthened by it, but also was willing to give up the good life of material blessings for a life of uncertainty and hardship in the land to which God directed him. What seems an even greater miracle to me is that Sarah, Abraham's beautiful and opinionated wife, was willing to give up the luxury of a beautiful home for a goat's hair tent in Canaan. Evidently, she did this without anger or resentment. Somewhere along the way she, too, must have learned the secret of silence.

The "eagle people" I've known in today's world differ in personality and interests, but they all have exhibited the quality of serenity in the midst of a busy and often difficult life. One such person was the late E. Stanley Jones, missionary to India and evangelist to America. Though I heard Dr. Jones's riveting sermons on many occasions, I was most influenced by reading some of the numerous books he wrote. I marveled at his physical stamina, his sustained energy, and his tremendous accomplishments right up until the time of his death.

Once, he preached for a week in the church where my husband was pastor and was a guest in our home. That week is still a shining hour in my spiritual journey. At one point, we asked the secret of his remarkably productive life. As he smiled, he replied, "I get my gasoline from the Lord." Then he said that he never missed his daily quiet time with God. After meditating on God's Word, it was a time of silent listening for his "marching orders." Then he told us that during the week of his graduation from seminary, he spent a whole night in prayer trying to discern exactly where God wanted him to serve. The young theologian had received three opportunities: to serve as pastor of a church, to be an evangelist for a Methodist conference, or to go to India as a missionary. Throughout the night, he read Scripture, thought, listened, and prayed. Yet it was not until the faint streaks of dawn appeared in the sky that God spoke to him through an inner voice, saying, "It is India." Dr. Jones's record of ministry on that continent and through his books, to believers and nonbelievers throughout the world, confirmed the authenticity of that call.

There is no substitute for being quiet and listening for God. It is only in our quietness that God can drop creative ideas and guidance. Once I heard a speaker say, "Boats don't come in on troubled waters." Likewise, amid distractions, noise pollution, and anxiety, our spirits falter. They soar only in a place of inner calm where we can focus and clarify our purpose. Then our spirits become lighter, freer, and more buoyant so that we can literally "lift off."

Our Minds Enable Us to Know God

Our minds are greater than the most sophisticated computers, but the secret is what we put into them. As the computer experts say, "Garbage in, garbage out." Pollution of the environment is a terrible thing, but pollution of the mind is even worse. Though we usually think of "mind pollution" as evil, violent, murderous, or pornographic thoughts, we can also pollute our minds with negative, fearful, resentful, and jealous thoughts. Such thoughts are like little termites that destroy the tranquillity of our minds and spirits.

Have you ever had trouble with termites? They are devious little creatures that will undermine your house as you walk around under the false assumption that everything is OK. I know a man who owned a house for less than a year when he discovered that the entire structure was ready to collapse because of termites. On the outside, the house looked great. It had just been painted before he purchased it. He also knew, from having lived in the same neighborhood, that the house had withstood a flood and a tornado. Yet, all the while, it was subtly being destroyed by the small, hidden creatures that "worked without ceasing."

In a similar way, people often go through the crises of life with flying colors. They take time to mourn traumas and tragedies but then move on constructively with their lives. Yet many of these same people all the while are being destroyed by mental termites.

Philosophers, psychologists, teachers, and religious leaders have disagreed about many things through the years, but they all seem to be in agreement about the importance of our thoughts. They often use six words as the determinative difference between success and failure: "You become what you think about."

Throughout history, many individuals have eloquently expressed the power of a person's thoughts. Marcus Aurelius, the great Roman Emperor, said: "The world in which we live is determined by our thoughts" (from *So Well Expressed* by H. George Bickerstaff, Salt Lake City: Bookcraft, 1968). William Shakespeare wrote: "Our doubts are traitors, and make us lose the good we oft would win, by failing to attempt" (from *Measure for Measure,* act I, scene IV). In our own country, beloved author and philosopher Ralph Waldo Emerson wrote: "A person is what he or she thinks about all day long" (from *So Well Expressed,* p. 112). Harvard sociologists and psychologist William James declared: "The greatest discovery of my generation is that human beings can alter their lives by altering their attitudes of mind" (from *Peter's Quotations: Ideas for Our Times,* compiled by Laurence J. Peter, New York: William Morrow Co., 1977, p. 318).

> *When Paul wrote to the Philippians that we should have the mind of Christ (Philippians 2:5), I believe he meant that we should be focused on God and not on ourselves. Only then can we tap into God's purposes.*

The Bible certainly confirms this belief in numerous passages. Here are a few examples:

- "As he [a person] thinketh in his heart, so is he." (Proverbs 23:7 KJV)
- "You reap whatever you sow." (Galatians 6:7 NRSV)
- "Whatever is true, whatever is honorable, whatever is just, whatever is pure, whatever is pleasing, whatever is commendable, if there is any excellence and if there is anything worthy of praise, think about these things." (Philippians 4:8 NRSV)

When Paul wrote to the Philippians that we should have the mind of Christ (Philippians 2:5), I believe he meant that we should be focused on God and not on ourselves. Only then can we tap into God's purposes and rise above pettiness, self-pity, anger, and even grief. I've found that filling my mind with God's Word gives me light in darkness and hope in despair. For example, one day a very good friend of our family had a massive heart attack and died instantly. We had just received flowers from him for a holiday celebration. The suddenness of his death left us in stunned grief. Yet the words of Jesus in John 14:1-3 instantly filled my mind and allowed my spirit to soar above my grief: "Do not let your hearts be troubled. Believe in God, believe also in me. In my Father's house there are many dwelling places. If it were not so, would I have told you that I go to prepare a place for you? And if I go and prepare a place for you, I will come again and will take you to myself, so that where I am, there you may be also" (NRSV).

It is through our minds that we come to know about God, and it is through our minds, as well as our hearts, that we make a commitment to God through Jesus Christ. When this commitment is authentic and we allow Christ to rule in every room of our lives, then the tremendous power of the Holy Spirit can guide and direct us. Because "eagle people" have learned to look for God, to wait quietly upon and listen for God, and to saturate their minds with thoughts of God, they can "run and not be weary, walk and not faint." They are able to live deeply, not quickly. In other words, they know how to catch the wind of the Spirit and soar like eagles!

Digging a Little Deeper

1. How do you react when the storms of life come? (Remember that you can't always choose what happens to you, but you can always choose your reaction.)

2. Read Isaiah 40:12-31. What does Isaiah tell us about the majesty and power of God? According to Isaiah, how can we limit God's power? Isaiah suggests that even the strongest among us will grow weary. What will refresh and empower us to "soar like eagles"?

3. Edwin Markham wrote these lines:

> At the heart of the cyclone
> . . . .
> Is a place of central calm.

That center, of course, is the eye of the storm. Have you known others who are able to live in the peaceful center even as the storm rages around them? Look honestly at your own life. Is it chaotic and fragmented, or have you learned to find peace amid the storms? If so, how?

4. God speaks to us most easily when we take time for silence. Read 1 Kings 19:11-12. When, or where, did God speak to a fearful and depressed Elijah? Respond to this statement: We can hear God's voice only when we make time for silence.

5. Read Matthew 8:23-27. How did Jesus calm the storm on the Galilean Sea? What assurance does this give us regarding his ability to bring peace to a fragmented spirit? What is required of us in order to receive this peace?

2
Give Yourself a Soaring Test

Consider it pure joy, my brothers, whenever you face trials of many kinds, because you know that the testing of your faith develops perseverance. Perseverance must finish its work so that you may be mature and complete, not lacking anything. (James 1:2-4 NIV)

One of the most interesting things I have learned about eagles has to do with their pattern of courtship. Generally, eagles do not fly in formation; but if a male eagle becomes interested in a female eagle, he begins to fly directly behind her. The female, understanding the overture, either will fly away if she is not interested or, if interested, will fly in circles around the male. Then, before there is a "marriage"—after all, eagles mate for life—the female gives a series of tests to her suitor. Smart eagle! First, the female eagle chooses a twig or small limb and throws it toward the ground. The male retrieves it and returns it to the female before it hits the ground. She repeats the test three or four times, and, with each test, she throws the twig closer to the ground. Although eagles have been clocked at two hundred miles an hour while making a dive, they occasionally miss the retrieve. In that case, the male eagle becomes ineligible as a partner for that particular female. (We'll see the reason for this important test at the end of the chapter!) If the male passes the test, a marriage ceremony occurs in midair as the "bride and groom" lock talons and turn somersaults. The only other time this ceremony occurs is when the last eaglet leaves the nest.

In many ways, this "marriage" of eagles is analogous to the marriage of human beings. Like the eagle's midair "dance," our weddings, too, are celebrations. Often the bride and groom feel as if they are in midair—on "cloud nine." Likewise, years later there is a time of rejoicing when the last child has successfully completed his or her education and leaves the nest. One thing we might learn from the eagle, however, is to be more intentional about giving each other a premarital "test." Perhaps if we did, there would be fewer couples whose wedding day dreams turn into nightmares.

I have laughingly said that my husband, Ralph, should have given me a practical test before we were married. He should have asked, "Can you cook?" Actually, I told him I couldn't cook before we were married, but he thought all girls said that so that the husband would be pleasantly surprised when his bride prepared their first meal. Well, Ralph was very surprised when I cooked our first meal!

My mother was an excellent cook, but she didn't like anyone else in the kitchen while she created her culinary delights. Though I cleaned house and washed what seemed like a billion dishes, I had never put a meal together. Three weeks before I was to be married, my mother was stricken in her conscience and taught me how to prepare one meal. It was a good southern meal: fried chicken, mashed potatoes, green beans, and orange congealed salad—the one with carrots, pineapple, and nuts.

Well, after we were married, we ate fried chicken, mashed

potatoes, green beans, and orange congealed salad for three weeks straight—except for breakfast when we had cereal and toast. I didn't even change the color of the gelatin. Even now, when we go to a covered dish dinner, my husband shies away from that orange gelatin. Fortunately for Ralph, I did learn to cook other meals!

Of course, a practical test having to do with one's cooking ability or other skills is not what I'm suggesting. The kind of test I mean is a careful examination of each other's values. Is each individual a person of integrity, responsibility, understanding, emotional maturity, and faith? And do they share the same set of values? When the apostle Paul wrote that Christians should not be unequally yoked by marrying an unbeliever (2 Corinthians 6:14), he was saying essentially that we must work from the same set of values in order to achieve harmony in marriage—especially when the storms of life are raging.

Why Do We Need to Examine Ourselves?

Like a marriage, the Christian experience is a journey of ups and downs, good days and bad days, successes and failures. And just as wise couples examine themselves in order to achieve harmony in marriage, so also we Christians should examine ourselves in order to achieve harmony with Christ; for only when we are in harmony with Christ are we able to soar above the difficulties of life. This self-examination—or "soaring test," if you will—can help us determine whether we have the necessary perspective and "equipment" for successful "soaring."

Here are some questions we should ask ourselves periodically:

The "Soaring Test"

1. *Am I comfortable in my ruts, or do I deeply desire to soar above my difficulties and live triumphantly?*
2. *Do I recognize that soaring requires discipline of body, mind, and spirit as well as persistence? Am I willing to pay the price? Are there negative emotions and self-destructive behaviors that are keeping me earth-bound?*
3. *Am I able to see myself as a person of worth, a child of God with infinite possibilities? If not, what is keeping me from claiming this identity?*
4. *Do I realize that I can soar only if Christ reigns within me, enabling me to soar on the wind of Christ's Spirit? Am I yielding daily to Christ in every area of my life?*
5. *What is the foundation of my life? What sustains me (holds me up, keeps me going) when difficulties come?*
6. *Do others see me living out my faith day by day?*
7. *How do I respond when the storms of life are raging all around me?*

It was Plato who wrote, "The life which is unexamined is not worth living" (Apology 38). The preceding questions are meant to help us in this examination—to help our deeds square with our words. Let me remind you, however, that our goal is not perfection, but integration through Christ into wholeness. This is not an instant accomplishment, but a lifelong process. We are, after all, Christians under construction. We are going to make mistakes, but thank goodness for forgiveness. If God can forgive Paul for killing all of those Christians before he "saw the light," then God can certainly forgive us if we truly repent and renew our commitment to lead a new life in Christ.

So, let us seek wholeness and excellence through Christ, but let us also enjoy the journey. The message of Jesus to the disciples in the first century is equally applicable to disciples in the twenty-first century: "I have told you this so that my joy may be in you and that your joy may be complete" (John 15:11 NIV).

Three Requirements for Soaring

When I think of persons who have overcome adversity, I always think of Job. Though he lived centuries before God was fully revealed to us in Christ, God gave Job the necessary resources for his time of testing. In the Old Testament book that bears his name, Job is portrayed as a wealthy man with upright character who loved God. The adversary (Satan) suggested to God that the only reason Job was righteous was that his life was full of so many good things—health, possessions, property, family, and cattle. If these were taken away, Satan believed that Job would forsake his faith in God. Though God didn't cause the calamities, he allowed them as a time of testing. God's faith in Job was vindicated!

Job experienced a series of successive catastrophes; he suffered boils all over his body (Job 2:7), and he lost all of his cattle, all of his money, and even his children (Job 13:1-22). His so-called friends accused him of disobeying God and thus receiving punishment from God. Job resisted this idea, knowing that he had lived his life in obedience to the God whom he loved. Even if God were punishing him, he said, he would not turn from God. His eternally significant words were, "Though he slay me, yet will I trust in him" (Job 13:15 KJV). Job's own wife finally told him to curse God and die. Although he was in the midst of a plethora of problems, he held steady in faith. What enabled him to do this? Let's consider three requirements for soaring that were evident in Job's life.

1. If you want to soar, you must build your life on the firm foundation of faith

Job was a man who feared God, walked uprightly, and worshiped each morning, offering sacrifices for his children (see Job 1–5). He built his life on the firm foundation of his faith. Later, in one of his parables, Jesus told the difference between building a house on the sand and building a house on the rock. When the storms come, the house built on sand collapses while the one built on solid rock stands firm (Matthew 7:24-27).

> ## Our lives need to be built on a "Rock of Gibraltar" kind of faith in God.

A friend of mine lived through Hurricane Andrew in 1992. She told of the terrifying experience of huddling with her family in a hall closet as windows were blown out and half of the roof was blown away. Yet, when the storm finally left the area and returned to the sea, their house was still standing while many of their neighbors' homes were left in shambles. The insurance appraiser assured them that the reason for their good fortune was a rock solid foundation.

As Jesus' parable illustrates, our lives need to be built on a "Rock of Gibraltar" kind of faith in God. As Christians, this faith is grounded in the person of Jesus Christ—a precious cornerstone, a sure foundation (Psalm 118:22 NRSV). The storms will come, and our windows may be blown out, but our lives will remain strong because we have built them on the firm foundation of faith. As the chorus of one of my favorite hymns says:

> On Christ the solid rock I stand,
> All other ground is sinking sand.
> (from "My Hope Is Built" in *The United Methodist Hymnal*, Nashville: The United Methodist Publishing House, 1995, p. 368)

This means, as Paul suggests, that Christ lives within us (Galatians 2:20). It means that we begin each day with Christ, asking, "Lord, what are we going to do today?" It means that as we study the Gospels and come to know more and more about Jesus, we begin to ask with each activity, "What would Jesus do?" It means that despite the complexity of life and the difficulty we have with some issues, we always seek to the best of our judgment and ability to follow the bold Galilean. It means that we no longer bog down in the "paralysis of analysis," but accept Christ's grace and seek to be instruments of his love. In private prayer and corporate worship, he affirms us and points to areas that need improving. If we ask, he forgives our shortcomings and gives us joy for the journey. Finally, as we end each day, we simply turn it back over to him with gratitude, not worry. Then our faith becomes not a religion, but a relationship—one that lasts for all eternity. There is no firmer foundation!

2. If you want to soar, you must "walk the walk"

Job not only "talked the talk"; he also "walked the walk." In other words, he lived daily on the principles that were included in his faith foundation (see Job 1:1-5). Edgar A. Guest was right on target in his poem "Sermons We See" when he wrote:

I would rather see a sermon than hear one any day.
I would rather see one walk with me than merely tell
    me the way.

> ## We Christians are the only "Bible" some people will ever read.

Once, as a young mother, I attended a women's retreat at our church. The leader was marvelous. She was inspiring, motivational, and practical in her suggestions. I could hardly wait until I could try her suggestions in all my relationships, especially those with our two preschool children. When the retreat ended, I had the privilege of driving the speaker across the city to her home. She was delightful company on the thirty-minute drive. Unfortunately, I had not driven out of the driveway before I heard her strident voice berating her children in anger. I felt almost sick at my stomach. Certainly I felt betrayed. She "talked the talk" in a convincing and professional manner, but one peek at her "walk" somehow negated her talk. We Christians are the only "Bible" some people will ever read. Our message is clear only if we walk in daily fellowship with Christ.

3. If you want to soar, you must hold fast to your faith in times of trouble

At the beginning of this chapter, I mentioned the tests that the female eagle gives the male eagle. There's a good reason why the female wants a male who can retrieve a twig before it hits the ground, and it has to do with her young. You see, after the baby eaglet is three months old, the mother eagle takes all of the soft leaves from the nest. The eaglet is disturbed and doesn't understand that this is the only way his talons can develop strength—not in a soft, comfortable environment, but in one that is difficult and harsh.

> *When life becomes too difficult for us and we feel as if we are falling, we must remember that "underneath are the everlasting arms" that restore us to safety.*

Later, the mother eagle takes the baby eaglet to the edge of the nine-foot nest. When the eaglet looks over, he is terrified and sees only death and destruction. The mother gives the eaglet a push out of the nest. The father eagle, who is flying in circles above the nest, never takes his eyes off his offspring. As the eaglet falls toward the ground, the father dives toward the earth and, using his wings, restores the eaglet to the nest. This continues until one day when the eaglet makes another attempt to fly, and his wings catch the wind. He begins to soar—indeed, to do what he was created to do.

When life becomes too difficult for us and we feel as if we are falling, we must remember that "underneath are the everlasting arms" (Deuteronomy 33:27 NIV) that restore us to safety. We may not understand our circumstances, but, like Job, we can know that God loves us with an unfailing love. Job did not understand why such terrible things were happening to him, yet he firmly believed that God's everlasting arms were undergirding him (see Job 13:15). As we continue to hold fast to our faith in God's unfailing love, relying upon the wisdom God gives us, we will eventually catch the wind of the Spirit and soar! Then we will become what we were created to be.

An Eagle Challenge

Recently, I received an E-mail from a beautiful young family who left the corporate world and are serving in sports ministry for the youth of Ethiopia. Though they have left behind many possessions that most of us feel are essential, they are learning new skills and are finding great happiness in their opportunity to serve Ethiopians in the name of Christ. They are soaring! Are you?

I challenge you seriously to ask God what he wants you to do with the rest of your life—and be willing to do it. Are you willing to turn loose the props that are holding you up and trust God for the future? If you fail at times (and we all will), remember that underneath are "the everlasting arms." God is our true refuge!

Digging a Little Deeper

1. Read John 10:10. Does this describe the way you are living at this period of your life? Why or why not?

2. Read Isaiah 40:31. If we are created to "mount up with wings as eagles" (KJV), why do you think we so often feel earthbound? Is it because we become comfortable in our ruts? List/discuss any ruts that are currently entrapping you. They may include things such as mindless television watching, selfishly refusing to be

engaged with life or the needs of others, being sabotaged by destructive habits due to a lack of discipline, and so forth. Try to be honest with yourself and face up to the deepest rut in which you are living. What can you do to get out of this rut?

3. Review Job 1–2. List/name each of the specific ways that Job was tested. How was Job eventually able to soar above these difficulties? What are the biggest problems you are facing at this time? Are you, like Job, able to soar above them, or are you bogging down in them, reacting in anger, or feeling hopeless? Read Job 42:1-6. What did Job come to realize?

4. Review the three requirements for soaring. What three things made it possible for Job to soar above his calamities? Are these three soaring requirements a vital part of your life? Do you believe it is ever too late for someone to build a solid foundation?

5. In Romans 5:3-5, Paul suggests that there are purposes in our difficulties and suffering. No one enjoys facing difficulties or being tested, but these are the times when we grow spiritually. Describe the times when you have grown the most spiritually. Were they times when everything was easy for you, or times when every fiber of your being was being stretched? Respond to the following statement: We were meant not for sedentary living, but for active engagement with life.

6. Just as the mother eagle pushes the eaglet out of the nest, sometimes God gives a "nudge." When has God called you to try something new that would use your talents in service to others? What happened? How might God be nudging you now?

3

Cultivate Three Key Characteristics

"I know the plans I have for you," declares the LORD, "plans to prosper you and not to harm you." (Jeremiah 29:11 NIV)

*T*his scripture verse from Jeremiah flashed through my mind as I watched the bald eagle fly effortlessly, almost playfully, through the unpolluted morning sunshine. Suddenly, however, when his razor sharp eyes spotted the object of his search (probably food), he became totally focused, wasting no time or energy as he dove toward the earth.

In retrospect, I realized that the eagle exhibited many attributes that are also present in "eagle people": self-confidence, self-discipline, focus, and faith. You might say that these characteristics were built into the very being of this magnificent bird—into the bone and wing structure that enabled him to soar. God created him with the wonderful capacity to soar. He didn't awaken every morning, wondering, "Is there a God?" or "Will I really be able to soar above obstacles, predators, and storms?" He instinctively knew that he could soar!

Like the eagle, we, too, were created to soar—perhaps not literally, but experientially. If we truly understand that God loves us unconditionally and with an everlasting love, we are "centered" within and have the unshakable confidence of faith. Jesus' death and resurrection are the exclamation points of this assurance. If we believe that God's plans are for our ultimate good, then no matter what the outward circumstances may be, we have an anchor for our souls and a real basis for positive confidence.

My friend Gemayel demonstrated this truth so graphically for me. She is a beautiful woman who has suffered unimaginably but has remained anchored, allowing her friends to witness how one can soar above life's difficulties. Though I didn't know her when she was married, I learned from others that she and her handsome husband were a poster couple for the perfect marriage, with two healthy, attractive children. In his travels, Gemayel's husband became involved with other women, leading to divorce and his immediate remarriage to a younger woman. Understandably, Gemayel experienced a brief period of depression at her husband's betrayal; yet despite all the chaos, she rekindled the bedrock Christian faith that had been a part of her childhood. She returned to the career she had pursued before the birth of her children. Despite her son's bouts with respiratory infections and her teenage daughter's brief period of rebellion, Gemayel stayed the course and reared two of the finest young people I have ever known—full of intelligence, productivity, faith, and self-confidence. She did this with little financial help from the children's father and no physical or emotional support. It was years before her friends knew of the excruciating pain she suffered from a previous back injury. Only after her children were safely established in their careers did she undergo the long months of multiple back surgeries and recuperation. Like the eagle, she exhibited self-confidence, focus, self-discipline, and faith.

Let's look at three key characteristics that enable us to soar like the eagle.

1. Eagle people are self-confident

Self-confidence is not arrogance or cockiness, but an appealing combination of knowing who and whose we are, humbly recognizing our strengths and limitations, and feeling "freed" by the spirit of Christ living within us. As the apostle John wrote, "If the Son [of God] sets you free, you will be free indeed" (John 8:36 NIV). This self-confidence can be seen in eagle people of all ages and vocations.

One of the stories from the September 11, 2001, tragedy involves a window washer. When the hijacked plane hit Tower One of the World Trade Center in New York City, all electrical power went out. On one elevator, there were six men: five executives and a window washer with a bucket and a squeegee. When the elevator stopped, the executives began to talk and disagree among themselves about what should be done. It was the window washer who emerged as the confident leader. He suggested that they use his squeegee pole to pry open the elevator door. By working together, they were able to force the door open. But they faced another obstacle. Before them was a white wall with the number fifty written on it. They were on an express elevator that didn't stop at certain floors, including floor fifty. Again it was the window washer who suggested that the sharp edge of the squeegee be used to break through the drywall. It was a wearisome task in which they, one by one, participated. Finally, there was an open wall, an escape to the street, and an opportunity to tell of their experiences. The window washer, who was proclaimed a hero and a leader, was not intimidated by the well-dressed, high-powered executives. Instead, he felt that he had the tools and the ability to get the job done (from "Could You Be a Leader?" by Daniel Goleman, in *Parade Magazine*, June 16, 2002).

> *Self-confidence is not arrogance or cockiness, but an appealing combination of knowing who and whose we are, humbly recognizing our strengths and limitations, and feeling "freed" by the spirit of Christ living within us.*

Dr. Nathaniel Brandon, renowned psychotherapist and pioneer in the study of self-esteem, has authored several books on the topic. In his book *The Psychology of High Self-Esteem*, he defines self-esteem as "feeling competent to face life and being worthy of happiness." Dr. Brandon says, "Life confronts us with many obstacles and challenges. If we feel confident, we will maximize our opportunities for success. If, on the other hand, we have low self-esteem, we set low expectations and give up too quickly" ("The Psychology of High Self-Esteem," a Nightingale Conant tape).

How do we build this kind of self-confidence? I believe the most important step is accepting ourselves as unique persons created in the image of God. When we surrender ourselves to the Lordship of Christ, we gain a healthy confidence in ourselves. This confidence is never self-glorification, or even the belief that our accomplishments lie only in our natural abilities. Rather, it is the recognition that our confidence is given by the power of the living Christ within us.

Recently I wrote a newspaper article about a college senior from an upper-income family who gave a large portion of her Christmas holidays to distribute humanitarian aid to children with AIDS in Uganda. She did this in the name of Christ. As she shared her spiritual journey with me, she said that her grounding in faith came through her parents. "They consistently showed the love of Jesus to each of their four children," she said. "Also, we had—and still do when we are home—a worship time when someone reads from the Bible and each of us prays." Then she told me that, in the summers of her sixth through ninth grades, she attended a Christian sports camp in Missouri where her commitment to the Lordship of Christ became a life choice. She told me, "The counselors were 'cool' adults who were good athletes, fun loving, and committed Christians. They modeled a confident lifestyle. At that pivotal time when peer pressure at school was mounting, I finally understood that this confident power was given through Christ living within me" ("God Gave Me a Heart for Service," *Chattanooga News Free Press,* February 22, 2003; *Kingsport Times News,* February 21, 2003).

The following suggestions may help you to cultivate *your* God-given self-confidence in practical, daily living:

Cultivating Self-Confidence

1. *Replace the fear of failure with positive affir-mations, such as "I can do all things through him who strengthens me" (Philippians 4:13 NRSV).*
2. *Distinguish who you are from what you do.*
3. *You may want to emulate some particular attribute in another person's life, but don't try to copy this individual. You are an original!*
4. *Insofar as possible, make peace with those who have wronged you.*

5. *Practice silence, Bible reading, and prayer for at least fifteen minutes each day.*
6. *Each night, empty your mind of worries. I try to do this as I undress and prepare for bed. I consciously breathe in the Holy Spirit and breathe out fears, worries, and resentments. I know that I can trust God with the night shift.*
7. *Cultivate friends who will help you grow.*
8. *Make a mental estimate of your assets and raise it 10 percent. Most people focus on their limitations rather than their strengths.*
9. *Make this daily affirmation: "From this day on, with the help of God, I'm becoming more and more conscious of all that is creative and positive. My life is becoming more Christ centered, more efficient, and more effective."*

One of the best reasons for cultivating self-confidence in these ways is that it results in focused and self-disciplined living.

2. Eagle people are focused and self-disciplined

When necessary, the eagle becomes completely focused for tasks such as securing food, taking food to the baby eaglets, or retrieving the eaglets when they fall. Here, he allows no distractions. How unlike the eagle most of us are! I've observed that when a latecomer enters church and walks down the aisle, more than half of the members of the congregation turn their attention away from the minister or the soloist and focus on the one who has interrupted the service. Perhaps one of the reasons for this is that we live in a fast-paced, technological society. We are accustomed to watching short segments on television, hearing instant news from around the world, surfing the Net, and communicating instantly through E-mail and FAX machines. I once received a "snail mail" letter from a friend who wrote, "I'm tired of E-mail. I type too fast and make too many mistakes. Not only that, but it is easier to express how I really feel and to know what the other person is feeling in a 'real letter.' It is also therapeutic to take time to reflect while writing." My sentiments exactly! Quick facts are great to send by E-mail, but thoughtful letters take more time.

Have you ever shaken hands with someone while he or she was waving and talking to someone else? It's exasperating! I'm convinced that our shortened attention spans can be corrected with three D's: desire, determination, and discipline. All of us have wished at one time or another that we could be less fragmented—that we could somehow "get it all together and remember where we put it." Wishful thinking is easy, but it brings no results. Deep desire, on the other hand, involves determination and commitment. I may casually wish I were ten pounds lighter, but unless I desire it enough to determine to increase my exercise and limit my caloric intake, it will not happen. Even then, after a good start, it won't happen without the third D: discipline. The discipline of day-by-day follow-through involves sacrificing some time, giving up excess refined sugars and saturated fats, and moving those muscles. Then it will happen! It's no different in any area of life. When we confidently focus on a specific goal or desired outcome, we must have desire, determination, and discipline to achieve it.

Three New Testament characters have taught me a great deal about focus and self-discipline. Jesus, of course, is our prime example. Even as a twelve-year-old boy, he was found by his parents in the temple at the Feast of the Passover, sitting among the elders, listening to them, and asking them questions. When his mother said, "Your father and I have been anxiously searching for you" (Luke 2:48 NIV), Jesus replied, "Why were you searching for me? . . . Didn't you know I had to be in my Father's house?" (Luke 2:49 NIV). The King James Version says, "Wist ye not that I must be about my Father's business?" From that point on, Jesus was focused on his mission: fulfilling God's purposes in the world. In the Lord's Prayer, he prayed: "Thy will be done in earth, as it is in heaven" (Matthew 6:10 KJV); in his Gethsemane prayer, he said, "Nevertheless, not my will, but thine, be done" (Luke 22:42 KJV); and even as he faced death, "he steadfastly set his face to go to Jerusalem" (Luke 9:51 KJV).

> *When we confidently focus on a specific goal or desired outcome, we must have desire, determination, and discipline to achieve it.*

Likewise, I think of the apostle Paul when I think of focus and self-discipline. After his conversion (Acts 9:3-18), Paul spent the rest of his life preaching the gospel and taking it outside the fertile crescent of the Middle East. To accomplish this gargantuan task was not a "walk in the park" for Paul. In his letter to the church at Corinth, he wrote: "Five times I received from the Jews the forty lashes minus one. Three times I was beaten with rods, once I was stoned, three times I was shipwrecked. . . . I have labored and toiled and have often gone without sleep. . . . I have been cold and naked. Besides everything else, I face daily the pressure of my concern for all the churches" (2 Corinthians 11:24-28 NIV). Despite all of this, Paul never lost his focus or disciplined sense of mission. We know this because he told the Philippians: "One thing I do: Forgetting what is behind and straining toward what is ahead, I press on toward the goal to win the prize for which God has called me heavenward in Christ Jesus" (Philippians 3:13-14 NIV). At the end of a life well spent, he was able to write to Timothy, his son in the ministry: "I have fought the good fight, I have finished the race, I have kept the faith" (2 Timothy 4:7 NIV).

Finally, I think of Priscilla. In Paul's travels, he lived for eighteen months in the home of Aquila and Priscilla in Corinth and established the Christian church there (Acts 18:1-4). Even in a day when women were seldom recognized and almost never given leadership roles, Paul chose Priscilla, along with her husband, to establish the church in Ephesus (Acts 18:18). Priscilla was an organizer and an encourager. She had the gift of wisdom and love in abundance. One of the evidences of this was the way in which she confronted the popular preacher Apollos. He preached only the baptism of John and didn't even know about Jesus. Priscilla knew that it was dangerous to tell only half the truth, hence, the confrontation. Obviously, it was her tact and humility of spirit that allowed Apollos to receive her words so well.

These three persons, Jesus, Paul, and Priscilla, would not have been able to fulfill their missions without focus and self-discipline. Yet it was their faith that allowed them to stay focused and disciplined.

3. Eagle people are full of faith

When I think of a person who was full of faith, I think of Abraham of the Old Testament (Genesis 11:23). Abraham—or Abram, as he was then called—didn't even know God except through oral stories about Adam and Eve and Noah. Yet, from his home in the Ur of Chaldees, he heard and heeded God's call, and Judeo-Christian history was forever affected. We read in Genesis

12:1-2, that God called Abraham to leave his home and go to a place where God would show him. To this seventy-five-year-old man, God promised to make of him a great nation so that the people of the earth would be blessed by him.

Through sharp testing and one incident that could have destroyed his family if it had not been for God's intervention (Genesis 12:14-20), Abraham remained faithful to God; and God kept his promises. This early biblical story is a beautiful example of walking humbly in faith before the living God.

> *"Jesus, help me, I don't think we are going to get out of this thing. I am going to have to go out on faith."*
> *—Todd Beamer, passenger on Flight 93, September 11, 2001*

When I think of a contemporary example of walking in faith, I remember Todd Beamer, the former Wheaton College graduate who was a passenger on the hijacked United Flight 93, which crashed in the Pennsylvania countryside on September 11, 2001. In a *Newsweek* story entitled "The Real Story of Flight 93," the author gave details from the cockpit voice recorder. Todd, like all the other passengers, was frightened. This was evidenced by the fact that he cried, "Jesus, help me, I don't think we are going to get out of this thing. I am going to have to go out on faith." The article reported that after the passengers were herded to the back of the jet, Beamer called the GTE Customer Center in Oakbrook, Illinois. He told the supervisor, Lisa Jefferson, that the passengers were planning to jump the terrorists and asked her to pray with him. Todd had a Lord's Prayer bookmark in his Tom Clancy novel, but he needed no prompting. He began to recite the prayer that Jesus taught his disciples (Luke 11:1-4), and Jefferson joined him.

Then Beamer and his fellow passengers prayed the prayer that has comforted millions in time of crisis: Psalm 23. No doubt these words must have been particularly comforting: "Yea, though I walk through the valley of the shadow of death, I will fear no evil: for thou art with me" (verse 4 KJV). Then came the famous last words: "Are you guys ready? Let's roll!" We know from the cockpit recorder that Beamer and other passengers wrestled with the hijackers. Evidence suggests that the hijackers crashed the plane to avoid a passenger takeover. Whatever happened, the hijackers' plans to fly the plane into the Capitol or the White House failed.

As Christians, we know that God can bring good out of evil. In Todd Beamer, the world witnessed a faith that held up in the extreme. It is that same faith that continues to bring comfort to Lisa Beamer, his young widow, and that sustains each of us through the ups and downs of life.

If we are going to soar over the obstacles in our lives like an eagle, we will need the characteristics of self-confidence, focus, self-discipline, and faith. Let us, then, as twenty-first-century disciples, regularly "draw near with faith" to God through Jesus Christ. We can do this through private prayer and corporate worship, through solitude and service, through joy and sorrow. Then our roots will be so deep in faith that we are not blown over by every wind or storm that comes our way. We will be able to hold steady in our difficulties and soar above them through the power of Christ. And Christ, through us, will encourage and inspire others.

Digging a Little Deeper

1. Read Jeremiah 29:11. What does this verse tell us? How do you feel about this?

2. God plans for eagles to soar, not just flap their gigantic wings with resultant fatigue or depression; but it is they who must do the flapping. What must *we* do in order to realize God's plans for

our good? What happens when we do not choose to follow God's plan?

3. We know some of the plans for our good that God has for us, such as loving one another as Christ has loved us (John 15:12). What are some other plans that you believe God has for your good? Read Matthew 19:26 and Matthew 28:20. Instead of feeling hopeless and alone, what does God want us to remember? Read John 14:27 and John 15:11. Instead of fear, anxiety, fragmentation, depression, and despair, what does God plan for us?

4. Read John 15:16. What does it mean to "bring forth fruit"? As a young person, I believed that God had only one plan for each of our lives, and that if we missed that, we were no longer in his will. As I grew older, I realized how narrow that view was. God does direct our lives if we are willing, but our call is to follow Christ and bring forth fruit in our world. Doors will open for us, and if we have the courage and faith to walk through, we may follow several careers while staying close to Christ. What doors of opportunity for service have you walked through, and with what results? What doors have you refused to enter, and with what results?

5. Of the eagle characteristics named in this chapter—self-confidence, focus, self-discipline, and faith—which do you most need in your life right now? Why?

6. Review/discuss the suggestions for cultivating self-confidence (pp. 40-41). Which do you most need?

7. Respond to this statement: Confidence is not arrogance, but the sure knowledge of our Christian heritage, made in the image of God (Genesis 1:27), redeemed by Christ (John 3:16), and, if we have accepted the gift, empowered by the Holy Spirit (John 1:12).

8. Read Psalm 8:5. What does this verse tell us about our heritage? What can we do to claim our heritage?

4

Don't Give Up When Life Says "No"

"I will not leave you comfortless: I will come to you." (John 14:18 KJV)

On February 1, 2003, I watched in horror as the space shuttle *Columbia* broke apart over Texas only fifteen minutes before it was to land at Kennedy Space Center in Florida. Immediately I thought of my friend June Scobee Rodgers. I could only pray that the family members awaiting their loved ones were as anchored in their faith as she and eventually could rise like a phoenix out of the ashes to triumph over tragedy.

Seventeen years earlier, on January 28, 1986, June stood exactly where those family members were standing. Her husband, Dick Scobee, was commander of the ill-fated *Challenger*. On that cold but clear January morning, she and her two grown children, Rich and Kathie, along with family members of the *Challenger* crew, watched with anxious anticipation. For Dick Scobee, Flight 51-L was the culmination of a lifetime dream, and June was grateful for that. In her book, *Silver Linings* (Macon, Ga.: Peake Road Press, 1996), she reports that as they waited for liftoff, her mind was filled with fond memories and unanswered questions. Then, after the expected flume of smoke and shaking of the earth caused by the raw power of millions of pounds of thrust, there was liftoff and wild cheering from onlookers. Only seconds later, as June reached to help Kathie with her baby, the unthinkable happened. The *Challenger* exploded into millions of pieces, claiming the lives of all seven courageous and well-trained crew members.

June's journey from unbearable tragedy—which makes you want to cry—to amazing triumph—which makes you want to cheer—is a moving testimony of God's awesome power to transform the human spirit. In the foreword to June's book, Dr. Robert Schuller writes, "You will see that faith can turn the darkest gloom into a bright cloud radiating with new life" (p. ix). As much as she would have liked to, June knew that she couldn't change the reality of the *Challenger*'s explosion. However, with the help of God, she could choose her reaction. Thankfully, she chose to bring good from a terrible tragedy in her life.

Steps to Take When Life Says No

With June's permission, I am sharing the steps that helped turn her "scars into stars." Perhaps these steps will help you face the future when life says no to you.

1. Allow yourself to feel the pain and experience the grief

Life can say no in many ways—through a big disappointment, such as the loss of a job or the betrayal of a friend, or a severe loss, such as the loss of a loved one through divorce or death. Regardless of the circumstance, one thing is certain: We must face the pain and deal with it. Despite our best attempts, we can't avoid it or short-circuit it. It's part of the process. You see, grief is a journey; and we must complete that journey if we are to be healed. It is like going from one city to another. We can't stop permanently in any of the small towns in between. Otherwise, we would never complete the journey.

All of us who have been through a grief journey know that it is not a straight path. There are peaks and valleys. One day we feel strong, and the next we dissolve in tears. I experienced this myself after the tragic loss of our twenty-year-old son, Rick. One day, many months after his death, I was shopping in a department store when a small tow-headed boy started running toward me. He looked exactly as our Rick looked at that age. Memories flooded my mind, and I burst into tears. I wasn't expecting that to happen, yet I really shouldn't have been surprised. Healing is not only an up and down process, but also one that takes time. Most grief counselors suggest that it takes at least one full year—during which one observes all the holidays and special days—before there is any real closure.

Disastrous results often occur when we try to short-circuit the grief journey. In her book *On Death and Dying* (New York: Macmillan, 1991), Elisabeth Kübler-Ross says there are certain stages we must go through if we are facing our own death or are grieving the death of a loved one. These stages include denial, anger, bargaining, depression, and acceptance. Actually, these stages often accompany any loss, including the loss of a job or relocation. My own experience has been that these stages don't necessarily come in any order. Sometimes they all seem to come in one day. At other times we linger too long in one stage, such as in depression. After Rick died, there were days when I literally had to make myself get out of bed and fulfill my responsibilities. Yet doing just that helped relieve the depression. Work for the hands to do helps heal a broken heart.

Although bargaining with God was never a temptation for me, I spent too much time saying, "If only." That kind of thinking is an exercise in futility and leaves you with unnecessary guilt. I also learned that it takes time for the emotions to catch up with what the mind accepts as reality. For example, I often caught myself setting Rick's place at the table and expecting to see him walk through the front door. It takes time for emotions to deal with a grim reality.

I know a man who was so lonely after the sudden death of his wife that he married a widow within four months. It was a disaster! Feeling that she was constantly compared with the first wife, the second wife was miserable. The man became depressed and withdrawn. Eventually they divorced. The man simply hadn't done his grief work.

Fortunately, June knew that she must allow herself to grieve, and she knew that it would take time; yet she had the additional pressure of having to grieve publicly. After all, the *Challenger* explosion was a national tragedy, and everyone was grieving. June remembers that while they were on a bus en route to the crew's quarters, they stopped at a red light. Cars were stopped everywhere. People were embracing each other; some were sobbing at their steering wheels. A wave of shock jolted across the land.

> *Grief is a journey; and we must complete that journey if we are to be healed.*

A similar phenomenon occurred after both the September 11 and *Columbia* tragedies. Families directly affected by each of these tragedies could no longer turn on the television without seeing the horrific events replayed again and again. They couldn't go to the grocery store without people crowding around them and talking; reporters camped outside their houses; there were no hiding places! For June, a breakthrough came when a friend offered her a lake house where only family and close friends could reach her; there she could begin to heal in private.

Although most of us never experience such a public grief experience, we, too, must allow ourselves the time and space to work through our grief in private. *How* we go about this differs from individual to individual. As I've learned from observation and personal experience, we each must handle our grief in our own individual ways. Yet, regardless of the different ways we work through our grief, there is One who is with each of us, helping us through the experience. In fact, it is my conviction that we can never attain acceptance until we believe in and trust this One who said, "I will not leave you comfortless: I will come to you" (John 14:18 KJV). When we allow Christ to have our time and our cooperation, he performs the miracle of restoring a broken heart.

2. Be centered in faith

We've considered in previous chapters how important faith is to our ability to soar above the difficulties of life. You might say that is the theme of this entire book. Yet there's a difference between having faith, or professing a belief in God, and being centered in faith, or living out that faith in daily life. When life says no, we need not only to have faith, but also to be centered in that faith. In other words, we need to have more than a professing faith; we need to have a *living* faith. I can't think of a better example than my friend June Scobee Rodgers.

Anyone who knows June knows that she has faith. Yet it is obvious that her faith is not a religion; it is a *relationship*—a relationship with Jesus Christ. In the time of crisis, she was not spiritually bankrupt. She had walked so closely with her Lord that she instinctively knew to turn to him for help. It was the Living Christ who brought peace to her wounded spirit and hope to her devastated heart.

> ### *We need to have more than a professing faith; we need to have a living faith.*

Through reading God's Word, allowing herself to be still, and praying, June could hear anew the words of Christ. Familiar verses took on a new depth of meaning—verses such as:

- "I am the resurrection and the life. He who believes in me will live, even though he dies; and whoever lives and believes in me will never die." (John 11:25-26 NIV)
- "Do not let your hearts be troubled. Trust in God; trust also in me." (John 14:1 NIV)
- "Peace I leave with you; my peace I give to you. I do not give to you as the world gives. Do not let your hearts be troubled, and do not let them be afraid." (John 14:27 NRSV)

You see, Christ understands our grief. He wept at the graveside of his friend Lazarus (John 11:34-35). Yet he doesn't want us to *wallow* in grief. He sends the Holy Spirit to comfort, direct, and empower us (John 14:15-20) so that we can walk into the future with joyful anticipation. And two of the most powerful ways that the Holy Spirit works in our lives are through Scripture and through prayer.

As June continued day by day to spend time reading God's Word and praying, she slowly began to relax, to sleep at night, to eat nutritionally, and to be centered in Christ's peace. It has been my experience that God, through the Holy Spirit, activates his Word in us, bringing about amazing results—relaxation where there has been tension; peace where there has been chaos; direction where there has been fragmentation.

As we walk the slippery slope of grief, the Holy Spirit not only steadies and directs us, primarily through the Word and prayer, but also brings wonderful surprises to help lighten our load. For example, June found her deceased husband's briefcase at the crew's quarters at Cape Kennedy. Inside was a Valentine's Day card "for my wife," with a very personal note to her.

I, too, experienced a much-needed surprise after Rick's death. Rick was buried on the Sunday before Thanksgiving. When Christmas came, we declined friends' invitations to share their Christmas dinner because we didn't want our presence to be a reminder of sadness that would dampen their joy. Instead, we invited our extended family and two church members who were without family to join us.

I had kept myself busily distracted with preparations, but as I took the turkey out of the oven, I felt as if I couldn't go through the dinner. "O God," I prayed, "I miss Rick so badly, and I wish he could be with us. My heart is aching. Please help me." As I was placing food on the dining room table, the doorbell rang. There stood a woman I had never seen before. "I have a Christmas gift from your son," she said. Then she produced the most beautiful hand-decorated wooden purse. Immediately I remembered the time I had commented that I needed a purse for our outdoor activities at the lake and on the boat. Written on the inside were these words: "Merry Christmas to Mother, from Rick." He had, after all, come home for Christmas!

I believe that reassuring surprises such as these are a part of God's wonderful serendipities. They help us know the presence of God in our everyday living. Even if we don't instinctively turn to Christ, as June Scobee Rodgers did, God in his compassionate mercy reaches out to us.

3. Lean into the future with action

After the *Challenger* disaster, many people throughout the United States wanted to erect a memorial statue to the crew. The families of the crew members, however, wanted to do something that would make a difference for others. They decided to con-

struct a series of living memorials where children could participate in simulated space flights and learn lessons in science and
math. June was named chair of that project. Today, there are
forty-six Challenger Centers in the United States, Canada, and
the United Kingdom. Since there is one in my home city, I have
seen firsthand the excitement of children as those future space
pioneers dream of going into space.

Today, seventeen years after the tragedy, June continues to lean
into the future with action. She not only is Founding Chair of the
Challenger Centers, but also is happily married to Army Lt.
General Don Rodgers, who is a knowledgeable, interesting, and
delightful man. Don, who lost his first wife to cancer, met June at
a sunrise service in Arlington Cemetery on Easter Sunday, 1988;
they were married a little more than a year later.

> *We are never to waste our tragedies,*
> *but are to use what we have learned to help*
> *others.*

June summarizes her philosophy of adversity with these
words:

> Even more important than being survivors, I think that God wants
> us to be winners. Only as we trust in a power that is greater than
> ourselves to provide the direction and give our lives meaning can we
> see the path that leads to our destination. Only through a closer
> walk with our Savior, Jesus Christ, can we have the courage to learn
> the lessons we need in the school of life. When we learn these
> lessons, we rise above our personal needs and turn to God for inspi-
> ration; then we can become dream makers for others, helping them
> find silver linings beyond their clouds. (*Silver Linings,* p. 143)

She obviously believes that we are never to waste our tragedies, but are to use what we have learned to help others. Some of the valuable lessons June has learned during the turbulent times of her life are universally relevant:

Lessons Learned in the School of Adversity

1. *As Matthews Arnold expressed it in his poem "To a Friend," "See life steadily and . . . see it whole"* (Norton Anthology of English Literature, *New York: W. W. Norton & Co., 1993*).
2. *Experience life without the clutter of anger, envy, fear, or guilt, which stifle and bog down our lives.*
3. *When one door is closed, God opens another. Dwelling on the past steals from us what is today and can be tomorrow.*
4. *The power of love can cause a magnificent phoenix to rise out of the ashes.*
5. *Keep humor and joy in your life.*
   (adapted from Silver Linings, *pp. 53, 87-90)*

We all can benefit from these life lessons, especially the reminder to keep humor and joy in our lives. I'll never forget a story involving June's college-age son, Rich. It seems that Rich was very protective of his mother, especially after the tragedy. Early one morning, the telephone rang and a male voice asked, "May I speak with June Scobee?"

Immediately, red flags went up for Rich. "Who is this?" Rich asked.

"This is the Vice President," patiently replied the voice at the other end.

Not to be deterred, Rich asked, "Vice President of what?"

"I am George Bush, Vice President of the United States."

A red-faced but still somewhat skeptical young man asked his mother, "Would the Vice President of the United States be calling you?"

"Yes, I missed his call yesterday," replied June as she reached for the telephone.

Later, when Rich graduated from the Air Force Academy in Colorado, his Commander in Chief was that very caller—now *President* George Herbert Walker Bush. Not only that, but the President also told that story in his speech. Yes, we all need to keep humor in our lives. Perhaps there's no better energizer for action and for serving others. Humor relieves tension, distracts us from pain, and enables us to be sensitive to the feelings and needs of others. In fact, when life says no, a sense of humor—along with intentional grieving, faith, and action—makes it possible for us actually to have the last laugh!

Digging a Little Deeper

1. Life says no in many ways—from disappointments as small as having rain when we had planned an outdoor event to something as major as losing a parent, a spouse, or a child by death. Reflect on/discuss some of the times when life said no to you. What helped you overcome?

2. Ask yourself this question: "If life said a big no to me today, would I be spiritually bankrupt?" If so, plan today to spend time in God's Word and in prayer. What else can you do to fortify your spiritual strength?

3. Reflect on/discuss times when we as a nation have been given a big no. How did we respond in each of those times?

Read 2 Chronicles 7:14-15. How can we prepare as a nation to meet another no in the future?

4. In what ways have you been made aware of the fragility of life? How has this awareness affected your interaction with family members and friends?

5. Find scriptural support for the following statement: Jesus lived his earthly life with his priorities firmly in order so that when a big no—rejection, persecution, betrayal, and crucifixion—came to him, he didn't panic. What are your priorities? Are they priorities in theory, or do you truly seek to live by them daily?

An Eagle Challenge

I have read that the people who accomplish the most are those who write down each evening the six most important tasks for the following day. As you begin to do this, you will have the opportunity to reflect on your true priorities and perhaps make some adjustments in your schedule or plans. For example, one Valentine's Day, instead of having an elegant dinner with my husband as we had planned, I decided to go with him, our son, and our daughter-in-law to a state high school wrestling match in which our grandson would participate. It is my least favorite sport, but loving and supporting my grandchildren is near the top of my priority list. I challenge you to think through your own priorities and try making a daily "top six" list.

5

You're Not Earthbound—
You Were Meant to Soar!

He lifted me out of the pit of despair, out from the bog and the mire, and set my feet on a hard, firm path and steadied me as I walked along. (Psalm 40:2 TLB)

ave you ever felt that you were in a miry pit and were being pulled down rather than allowed to soar? Once, when Ralph and I were in Florida, we drove past a deserted area of a beautiful white, sandy beach. Since we had an hour before joining friends for dinner, both of us said simultaneously, "Let's go sit on the beach and enjoy the sunshine."

In order to reach the beach, however, we had to walk through a section that looked a little like a marsh. No problem! We kept running shoes in the car, and it didn't matter if they got muddy. We'd simply slip back into good shoes on our way to dinner. Little did we know what awaited us. As soon as I stepped into the strange looking sand, I knew why the beach was deserted. "It's quicksand!" I shrieked as I began to sink. When Ralph reached to help me, he became engulfed, too.

In retrospect, we are sure that passing motorists must have found our scene hilariously funny, but it was deadly serious and scary to us. Alternately, we were clutching each other, sinking, screaming, and finally being pulled free by the sheer strength of Ralph's six-foot-two body. Since then, I never read the second verse of Psalm 40 without thinking of our experience with quicksand.

Another memory comes to mind when I read Psalm 40:2. The year was 1957, and Ralph had done a pulpit exchange with a minister from Auckland, New Zealand. It is a country of spectacular beauty. On its two small islands are the fjords of Norway, the beaches of the South Pacific, and the Alps of Switzerland. We were fortunate to be there during their summer, and the weather was glorious. It seemed that every family in Auckland owned a sailboat!

We came to love the New Zealanders, especially the members of our Auckland church, who blessed our lives in so many ways. We still smile when we think of the beautiful reception given in our honor as we completed our two-month sojourn among them. The decorations were creative, the skits were funny and touching, and the choir even sang "The Tennessee Waltz" and "Rocky Top" for us!

One thing, however, puzzled us about that land on the other side of the world: Their national bird is the kiwi. The kiwi cannot fly and doesn't like light. In fact, it only comes out at night. How like that bird we sometimes are! Unfortunately, some of us have settled for being kiwi people rather than the eagle people we were meant to be.

You Don't Have to Be a Kiwi Forever

Kiwi people are good people who long to soar like the eagle people they admire, yet they remain earthbound. Why? Most of the kiwi people I know are hindered by destructive habits or negative emotions. Of course, there are times in our lives when each of us is a kiwi temporarily, such as when we encounter unexpected difficulties and suffering. Twice in my own life, I was a kiwi for a while: first, when our son Rick died, and later, when I underwent months of chemotherapy following the removal of an ovarian tumor. Since my mother and grandmother both died of ovarian cancer, I was overwhelmed by anxiety. In both of those hard places in my life, I certainly didn't soar, and I couldn't even run well for a while. Yet I was able to keep on going because I knew the truth of Isaiah 40:31: "Those who hope in the LORD will renew their strength. They will soar on wings like eagles; they will run and not grow weary, they will walk and not be faint" (NIV). I learned that if I was going to avoid being a kiwi forever, if I was going to break from the miry pit, I must practice the art of "bounce-back ability," which we will discuss later in the chapter.

Like sinking in quicksand, it's easy to become bogged down in the kiwi lifestyle; yet we must avoid it at all costs! Let's take a look at some of these common "traps" that can prevent us from soaring.

1. Kiwi people have destructive habits

All kiwi people, like eagle people, have the *capacity* to soar. Some kiwi people, however, remain earthbound by cultivating destructive habits that keep them chained in defeat.

Comparison

Each year since 1997, more than one million individuals have filed for bankruptcy in the United States. In 2002, the number was

1,240,012 (statistics from the Administrative Office of the U.S. Courts, Statistical Tables for the U.S. Government). For many of these individuals, bankruptcy was not the result of an unexpected hospitalization or a tragic accident. Instead, it was the result of a consumer mentality—wanting more and more things without counting the cost of cumulative interest payments. It's a matter of keeping up with the Joneses—the hypothetical family who lives down the street in a larger home. In his book *The Secret of Radiant Living* (London: Hodder & Stoughton, 1957), Dr. William E. Sangster suggests that we might be able to keep up with the Jones family in our neighborhood, but there will always be a family of Joneses who have a larger house and a more expensive automobile. To allow another person or family to determine our lifestyle is not only energy-depleting and foolish; it also can have deadly consequences.

The doctor who delivered our first child was an excellent gynecologist, having taught and practiced in one of the finest medical schools in our nation. He had moved to our city less than a year earlier and had bought a large home in an upper-income neighborhood.

On a Friday, Ralph accompanied me to the doctor's office for my six-week checkup, and during that visit he learned that the doctor and his family had not affiliated with any church. That very afternoon, Ralph called a pastor friend who had a church in the doctor's neighborhood. The friend promised to visit the doctor's family on Monday.

Tragically, it was too late! After having been turned down for another loan by a bank, the doctor and his wife took their lives on Saturday evening in their bedroom, leaving his mother, whom they had invited to visit for the weekend, with their children. What a terrible loss! They deprived their children of a normal family life; they deprived our community of their many skills and talents; and they deprived this grandmother of the joys of being a grandparent, placing on her an almost unbearable burden—all of this because they had not counted the cost.

In Luke 14:28, Jesus tells us, "Suppose one of you wants to build a tower. Will he not first sit down and estimate the cost to see if he has enough money to complete it?" (NIV). For the Christian, sound planning is essential in financial as well as spiritual matters. The first step is to give thanks for our blessings, including the privilege of life, and keep our eyes upon Jesus without comparing ourselves with others.

The destructive habit of comparison is also evident in our society's obsession with physical appearance. Each year, Americans spend billions of dollars on personal hygiene products and cosmetics, clothing, accessories, and plastic surgery. For many, physical appearance has become the priority of life.

> *The prophet Samuel reminds us, "The LORD does not look at the things man looks at. Man looks at the outward appearance, but the LORD looks at the heart" (1 Samuel 16:7 NIV).*

Several years ago, I spoke for a singles' conference in a church in Atlantic City, New Jersey, during the week of the Miss America pageant. I soon learned that most of the pageant contestants were staying in the same hotel I was staying. When I first walked through the lobby full of these five-foot-nine-inch beauties, I felt vertically challenged (at five feet, two inches) and overweight (at 108 pounds)! Fortunately, I've lived long enough to appreciate the fresh beauty of those girls without becoming riddled with envy or jealousy. During the conference, I talked about a far more enduring kind of beauty—a beauty of character, based on Christian values; a beauty of relationships, based on the love of Christ; and a beauty of spirit, based on Christ's living within us. As the prophet Samuel reminds us, "The LORD does not look at the things man looks at. Man looks at the outward appearance, but the LORD looks at the heart" (1 Samuel 16:7 NIV).

Addictive behavior

Last year, a longtime friend of mine died after years of physical abuse to her body. I first met Katie in happier times. She was happily married, had four beautiful children, and was active in her church and community. She was creative, loving, and a very loyal friend. Then, there was a series of difficulties in her life—the loss of a child, financial problems, and stress in her marriage.

Rather than facing her problems head-on, she escaped by using alcohol and tobacco. When friends saw an addictive pattern developing, we tried everything we could think of to help—having confrontational talks with her, planning an intervention of family and friends, taking her to see a counselor, and strongly encouraging her to enter a rehabilitation facility. Nothing seemed to help until her health got so bad that she was frightened into giving up her life crutches. But it was too late! Her unnecessarily early death robbed her of the joys of healthy living and watching her grandchildren grow to maturity. Tragically, Katie didn't count the cost as she built her house of life.

There are many other addictive behaviors that can derail our lives and rob us of healthy and happy living. Among these are excessive overeating, sexual promiscuity, extramarital affairs, lying, cheating (on everything from college exams to income tax reports), and gambling. One of the participants in the singles' conference I mentioned earlier was a social worker, and she told me that a high number of people who come to Atlantic City to gamble remain there because they become homeless, forcing their families to go on welfare. They became addicted to the belief that they could get something for nothing.

Generally speaking, addiction is the result of trying to escape our problems and difficulties. Many people try to short-circuit the pain by taking what they consider to be the easy way out. Unfortunately, they usually end up self-destructing. They need to know that Jesus spoke truthfully when he said, "I am the way, and the truth, and the life" (John 14:6 NRSV). The life he gives, when we invite him into our hearts, is for the "here and now" as well as for eternity.

2. Kiwi people have negative emotions

Some kiwi people remain earthbound because they don't realize that negative emotions actually trap them in the "miry pit"— what I call the quicksand of life. Giving in to negative emotions can become so habitual that eventually we find we are chained to the pit! Let's look at some of the destructive emotions that can chain us.

Negativism

Negativism, or pessimism, seems to be the mother of many destructive emotions. This is not hard to understand when we consider that we are bombarded daily by the media with news of unrest, violence, and terrorism. If we choose to fill our minds with a steady diet of these thoughts, we fall prey to and become inundated by negativism. We become pessimistic, unhappy people who actually drain energy from those around us.

On the first day after leaving intensive care following my cancer surgery, a woman I had never seen before sailed into my room, acting as if she knew me well. Struggling to think in what context I had known her, I decided that the surgery must also have affected my brain.

"Tell me where I have known you," I said weakly.

"Oh, I read your newspaper column every week," she replied jauntily.

At first I tried to focus, though somewhat hazily, on her conversation. When she went from jaunty to negative, however, I could actually feel energy flowing from my body. She told in gory detail about her friend who had a similar cancer to mine. It was when she started telling about her friend's death and funeral that I interrupted, saying, "I'm sorry, but I am very tired and need to rest." I rang for the nurse, who came promptly into the room and invited the thoughtless woman to leave. I was "wiped out," and it took me hours to regain my strength.

For many people, negativism has become an "unconscious" and habitual thought pattern. Often this thought pattern develops early in life because of a negative childhood environment. In any case, you *can* interrupt the pattern. How? By changing your thoughts! Yes, we have the power to change our thought patterns. The rubber band trick can help. Once, during a negative period in my life, I wore a rubber band around my wrist for months. Every time I even thought a negative thought, I would pull back the rubber band and let it sting my wrist. It got my attention, and gradually I changed. It took time, effort, and prayer, but it worked.

Paul must have understood the destructive power of negativism because he wrote to the Philippians, "Let the same mind be in you that was in Christ Jesus" (Philippians 2:5 NRSV), and "Whatever is true, whatever is honorable, whatever is just, whatever is pure, whatever is pleasing, whatever is commendable, if there is any excellence and if there is anything worthy of praise, think about these things" (Philippians 4:6 NRSV).

Negativism can poison our relationships, rob us of energy and motivation, and enable misery to cover our lives like a veil. Yet negativism comes from our thoughts, and we can change our thoughts. We may not be what we think we are, but what we think, we are! So, "let the same mind be in you that was in Christ Jesus" (Philippians 2:5 NRSV).

Worry

Worry is another negative emotion that keeps us in inner turmoil, depleting energy that could be used for constructive living. The Anglo-Saxon word for worry means "to strangle." If you ever have been really worried about something, you know that this meaning is right on target! You feel as if you can't breathe. "I'm worried sick" is another apt description. Worry is the misuse of imagination.

Mark Twain said that he had known a lot of troubles in his life, and most of them had never happened. I remember reading about a businessman who decided to analyze his worries. He said that 40 percent of them were likely never to happen; 30 percent stemmed from situations in the past that could not be changed; 12 percent concerned criticisms from other people, which he said didn't really matter; 10 percent were about his health, which he was already doing his best to protect; and only 8 percent were legitimate concerns.

In his book *The Workbook on Coping as Christians* (Nashville: Upper Room Press, 1988), Maxie Dunnam says that worry is negative, and concern is positive. Concern, then, is seeing the problem from a clear perspective and then taking positive action to correct it. If you can't do anything about the problem, you need to turn it loose.

> *Instead of allowing our minds to go around and around one subject like a song getting "stuck" on one note, we should interrupt the pattern and pray.*

One of the scripture passages that continues to help me when I catch myself needlessly worrying is Philippians 4:6-7: "Do not be anxious about anything, but in everything, by prayer and petition, with thanksgiving, present your requests to God. And the peace of God, which transcends all understanding, will guard your hearts and your minds in Christ Jesus" (NIV). Basically, Paul is saying that instead of allowing our minds to go around and around one subject like a song getting "stuck" on one note, we should interrupt the pattern and pray. Interestingly, he suggests that whatever the problem, we should first give thanks.

Once, while speaking on this passage, I said that no matter how difficult a situation is, we can always find at least one good thing in it. I suggested that we should start giving thanks for that one thing because it will break the logjam of worry and anxiety, allowing Christ to pour in his insight and power and peace. A woman in the audience who was grieving the recent death of her husband later told me that she couldn't think of one good thing in her situation. That evening, however, she thought of my suggestion and wrote down these words: "I am thankful that I no longer have to listen to Howard Cosell announce football." She told me that she had laughed for the first time since her husband's death, knowing how much he would have laughed at her comment. The emotions that had jelled into a hard knot of pain in her heart seemed to dissolve. She laughed and cried and even felt hope rising within her. That night she slept peacefully.

Gratitude opens our hearts to God's power.

Jealousy

Jealousy, another deadly negative emotion, is the backwash of personal insecurity. If allowed to continue, jealousy can devastate friendships, destroy marriages, overload our minds with stress, and keep us from the jobs, people, and opportunities we most desire. No wonder it is called "the green-eyed monster"!

An Eagle Challenge

List your worries on a piece of paper. Now, analyze each of them. Are you wasting your energy on a past or imagined event? Do you feel "strangled" by a given problem, or are you able to see it from a clear perspective? Prayerfully consider what positive action you can take to correct the problem. Write it down. If you are unsure, consult a trusted Christian friend, a Christian counselor, or a pastor. Then, whether or not there is something you can do, turn the problem over to God in prayer with thanksgiving. Believe that God is in control and will give you peace.

I know a middle-aged man who is so jealous of his wife that she feels imprisoned, as if she is suffocating. If she even speaks to another man at a social gathering, her husband is certain that something sexual is going on between them. She has to account for every minute of her time. If she is even fifteen minutes late, he goes into an anxiety attack. There is nothing rational about his behavior. Though his wife is attractive, she is not a glamorous beauty. She is a kind, loving wife and mother who is one of the finest Christians I have ever known.

There came a day, however, when the wife had "had it," and she told her husband that either he would see a Christian counselor, whom she had tried, unsuccessfully, to get him to see earlier, or she would leave until he did. Recognizing the determination in her voice, he finally saw the counselor. Although it took a long time and much patience on the part of both husband and wife, he received great mental as well as spiritual help. The counselor discovered that there had been instability in this man's boyhood home, in which there had never been trust. Even more damaging was an affair that he had had with a married woman before he and his wife were married. The ever-present guilt was consuming him and causing him to project the lust he had experienced onto his wife's motives. His greatest breakthrough came when he confessed the affair to his wife and to God and received forgiveness from both. His new commitment to the living Christ enabled him to begin to see his own strengths and to handle his old jealous thoughts when they occasionally resurfaced. Today their home is a completely different environment. Where jealousy once was paramount, now trust and love abound.

The biblical character who comes to mind most readily when I think of jealousy is Saul, who was Israel's first king (1020 B.C. to 1000 B.C.). The first indication of Saul's jealousy came after young David defeated Goliath. At first, King Saul was pleased with David and invited him to live in his house. When the battle against the Philistines was finally over, however, women lined the streets, shouting, "Saul has slain his thousands, / and David his tens of thousands" (1 Samuel 18:7 NIV). Saul's pride was hurt, and his anger flared against David.

Twice Saul sought to kill David by throwing a javelin at him as the young shepherd played the harp. Saul's jealousy grew so intense that David had to go into exile, constantly fleeing from the king's wrath. Eventually, Saul's jealousy destroyed every ounce of his own peace of mind and happiness and made him a mad monster. At the same time, Saul's anger prevented David from enjoying his home and family and learning from the king whom he would succeed. You can read the entire story for yourself in 1 Samuel 15–31.

Another example of the long-term and corrosive effects of jealousy is found in the book of Genesis, chapters 11–23. Here we read the story of Abraham, whom God called to become the head of a great nation, and his wife, Sarah. For the most part, we remember the good things about Sarah—her willingness to follow God's command to leave her home and live for years in goat-hair tents in the desert; her beauty and strength; the way her husband, and later her son, adored her. Yet there are two episodes when her jealousy strained her marriage and destroyed her peace.

First, Sarah was frustrated when she was unable to give her husband a son, and she insisted that he take her Egyptian maid, Hagar, as a concubine to bear a child. Because this kind of thing was often done in their culture, and many marriages were ones of convenience, this was no big deal. But Abraham and Sarah loved each other deeply, so the arrangement resulted in conflict between the two women. When Hagar became pregnant, she became arrogant and disrespectful of her mistress. Sarah, in her anger and jealousy, so mistreated Hagar that the girl left. In the desert, Hagar thought she was going to die, but God provided water and sent her back to serve Sarah (Genesis 16:1-11).

> *Jealousy always has been, and always will be, based on fear—the fear of losing someone or something we feel should be ours. . . . The irony is that in each of these situations, the real enemy is not our "competitor" but ourselves.*

Later, after Sarah's own son, Isaac, had been born, she became extremely jealous when Hagar's son, Ishmael, teased Isaac. She was so angry that she asked Abraham to banish Hagar and Ishmael to the desert. Once again, God protected them and promised that Ishmael would become the leader of another group of people—the Arabs. Even today, the strife and conflict between the Arab and Israeli nations continues—perhaps the unfortunate results of Sarah's jealousy.

Jealousy is just as disastrous to Christians in the twenty-first century as it was to Saul and to Sarah. Jealousy always has been, and always will be, based on fear—the fear of losing someone or something we feel should be ours, such as a job, a part in a play, a position in the community, a boyfriend or girlfriend, a husband or wife. The irony is that in each of these situations, the real enemy is not our "competitor," but ourselves.

Recently, a beautiful woman in her late thirties came to talk with me about the fact that she was about to lose the second man to whom she has been engaged—all because of her clinging, possessive, and jealous manner. She simply does not see herself as a beautiful, talented woman worthy of love—worthy because she is made in the image of God; she has been redeemed by Christ; and, when she accepts this gift of redemption, she will be empowered by the Holy Spirit. She needs to discover the radical freedom that comes when Christ becomes Lord—not just a casual "friend" in our lives. When she learns this, she will know the truth that will set her free.

Jealousy kills spirits, destroys marriages, mars in-law relationships, poisons friendships, and generally causes misery in the lives of all those who fall into its clutches. What can we do to stop this green-eyed monster? We must rediscover the meaning of Christian love; and nowhere is it expressed as succinctly and beautifully as in the thirteenth chapter of the letter to the Corinthians, called the love chapter. Whenever the "monster" rears its ugly head, let us reread the love chapter and meditate on its wisdom, asking God to fill our hearts with divine love.

Breaking Out of the Miry Pit

Of course, there are many other negative emotions that can keep us in the miry pit, though we may sincerely desire to soar—emotions such as fear, uncontrolled anger, prejudice, and resentment to name a few. But there is good news: We *can* break out of the miry pit! How? The solution is to face our difficulties honestly and positively through the power of Jesus Christ. Through Christ, we are able to build what I call "bounce-back ability."

In my book *Build Your Bounce-Back Ability* (Nashville: Dimensions for Living, 2000), I explained that when tragedy or difficult times come, we can react in one of four ways. First, we can choose to react like an uncooked egg when it is dropped on the floor: It breaks and splatters everywhere. Unfortunately, some people remain "splattered" emotionally for years. Second, we can choose to react like an orange when it is dropped: It doesn't splatter but hits the ground with a thud, stopping where it has fallen. Like the orange, we can put our lives on hold and refuse to move on. Third, we can choose to react like an apple when it is dropped: It hits the ground and keeps on rolling, but it is badly bruised on the inside. Some people go back to work very soon after a tragedy, and unless you know them well, you wouldn't even realize that they are hurting terribly inside. Or, finally, we can choose to react like a live tennis ball: The harder it hits, the higher it bounces back!

I am convinced that the latter reaction is possible only through a personal relationship with Jesus Christ. That doesn't mean that we don't feel the pain or need to grieve. We do! Yet, as we read God's Word, pray, and walk in fellowship with Christ day by day, we are given hope, and even joy, for the journey. And as our hope and joy increase, we are able to loose the chains that have bound us and break out of the miry pit, soaring into the victorious and abundant life that God intended for us.

An Eagle Challenge

Are you in a miry pit? If so, how can you break free of the entrapments that are keeping you from soaring? This line from the hymn "Spirit Song," by John Wimber, summarizes for me the first actions we need to take: "Let him [Christ] have the things that hold you" (The United Methodist Hymnal, *Nashville: The United Methodist Publishing House, 1995, p. 347). Take time now to consider prayerfully your own situation and write a plan of action. Be as specific as you can, listing each of the steps you need to take. Seek the help or advice of a pastor, counselor, or other qualified professional as necessary. Remember that with the help of God, you can overcome and soar!*

Digging a Little Deeper

1. Read Psalm 40:2. Are you now, or have you ever been, in a miry pit of despair like the psalmist? Why? Reflect or discuss.

2. In what way(s) are you feeling earthbound like a kiwi? Is a destructive habit, a negative emotion, or a lack of faith keeping you from soaring?

3. Has the destructive habit of comparison crept into your life? Are you trying to keep up with "the Joneses"? If so, what motivates you—materialism, envy, ego? How can you use your unique abilities and God-given potential to become the best per-

son you can be—an original rather than a cheap copy of someone else?

4. Respond to the following statements: An addiction stems from a desire or a craving that, if indulged, becomes a destructive habit. A destructive habit puts your life "out of balance," hurting you and your Christian witness. Do you have an addiction to anything—television, food, drugs, alcohol, tobacco, gambling, sex, exercising? What have you tried to overcome this/these addictive behavior(s)? What have been the results? What next steps do you think you need to take?

5. Do you know anyone who is guilty of negativism? What do you think accounts for this? What observations or insights can you draw from this person's example? Generally speaking, are you more negative or more positive? To be sure, write down all of your reactions for a given day (including mental reactions). You may be, as I was at one time in my life, totally surprised to find out how negative you really are. If so, determine to change! Learn to interrupt negative thoughts (use the rubber band trick as a reminder; see p. 66); learn and regularly repeat some positive affirmations from the Bible; and pray, knowing that the Holy Spirit will empower you to embrace positive hope and joy.

6. Do you consider yourself to be a "worrier"? Why or why not? Remember that worry is like sitting in a rocking chair: You may be moving, but you are going nowhere! Follow the Eagle Challenge at the conclusion of this chapter, writing down an action plan for each of your worries.

7. When have you fallen prey to jealousy, the green-eyed monster? What evoked your jealousy, and what helped you overcome it? Which of the Old Testament characters discussed in this chapter do you most identify with: King Saul or Sarah? Why?

8. Read Isaiah 40:31. Recall those times when you have been able

to "soar like an eagle" and "run and not be weary." What helped you most in these times? Stop now to give thanks and praise—privately or with others.

9. Reflect on/respond to this statement: Only a close, daily relationship with Christ will allow you to bounce back from the difficulties you encounter and, subsequently, to soar like an eagle.

6

Learn to See the Big Picture

Do you have eyes but fail to see, and ears but fail to hear? (Mark 8:18 NIV)

As a young adult, I was invited to be member of a committee charged with the responsibility of working through a very controversial issue in our civic club. When time came for the meeting to begin, the chairman said, "Bill is on the way but will be a few minutes late. If it is all right with you, I'd like to wait to begin until he arrives. After all, he is the one with 'eagle eyes.'"

Of course, the committee members gave approval to delay the meeting until "eagle eyes" appeared. It was the first time I had heard the phrase used to describe a person. At home that evening, I went straight to the dictionary and the encyclopedia to learn more about the eagle's eyesight. I discovered that eagles have four to eight times better eyesight than human beings. In fact, what humans can see from thirty yards, eagles can see from two hundred yards. These birds also have two centers of focus that allow them to see both forward and sideways at the same time (*Eagles:*

Masters of the Sky, ed. Rebecca L. Grambo, Stillwater, Minn.: Voyageur Press, 1999). I realized that the phrase "eagle eyes" is meant to describe someone who can see the whole picture with clarity and focus.

Since then I've learned more interesting facts about the eagle. Bald eagles are capable of seeing fish in the water from several hundred feet above while soaring, gliding, or flapping in flight. This is quite a feat since most fish are countershaded, meaning that they are darker on top and thus harder to see from above. Fishermen confirm how difficult it is to see a fish just beneath the surface of the water from only a few feet away (www.baldeagleinfo.com). This phenomenon is possible partly because eagles have large photoreceptors in the retina. A flatter cornea than those in humans enables eagles to keep the total visual field in focus simultaneously (*How Animals See: Other Visions of Our World,* by Sandra Sinclair, New York: Facts on File Press, 1985). In addition, eagles have two sets of eyelids. The inner set serves as "sunglasses," allowing the eagle to fly into the light of the sun. The inner eyelids, or nictitating membrane, slide across the eye from front to back, wiping dirt and dust from the cornea. Because the membrane is translucent, the eagle can see even while it is covering the eye.

My study of these unusual birds has made me more aware than ever before that all creatures great and small are, in the words of the psalmist, "fearfully and wonderfully made" (Psalm 139:14 NRSV). Though our physical eyesight will never be as keen as the eagle's, God has given us wonderful gifts and abilities that enable us to have "eagle eyes"—to see the big picture with clarity and focus. Let us consider some of the ways God wants us to use this capacity for eagle eyesight for the benefit of his kingdom.

You Can Use Your "Eagle Eyes" to Know the Truth

When Jesus and the disciples were crossing to the other side of the Sea of Galilee, the disciples discovered that they had only one loaf of bread. As they continued to worry and talk about it, Jesus chided them by saying, "Do you have eyes but fail to see, and ears but fail to hear?" (Mark 8:18 NIV). After all, they had just witnessed Jesus feeding the multitudes with five loaves and two fish, as well as other miracles, and still they were preoccupied with matters of the moment. It was as if Jesus said to them, "Have you been with me so long and still don't understand that I am God's anointed one, the Messiah? You have eyes but you don't see the truth, and ears but you don't hear it." In essence, Jesus was asking if experience had taught them anything.

Unfortunately, we're no different. Most of us learn only the negative lessons of experience. Too often our experiences cause us to view life with pessimism or resigned hopelessness. We forget there are positive lessons to be learned in every circumstance. We need to use our "eagle eyes" to see the truth of the big picture. We need to remember that sorrow came, and we got through it; temptation came, and, somehow, we didn't fall; illness came, and we recovered; a problem seemed insoluble, and, somehow, it was solved; we reached the breaking point, and we didn't break. Are we blind to the fact that there isn't anything that God can't bring us through? Do we have eyes but do not see?

> *Most of us learn only the negative lessons of experience. . . . We forget there are positive lessons to be learned in every circumstance.*

The biblical character of Elijah, the Tishbite, illustrates how even a strong believer can see God's mighty works and then immediately fall into pessimism. There is a wonderful story about Elijah in 1 Kings 18–19. Since there had been no rain for months, Elijah challenged the 450 prophets of Baal to a contest on Mt. Carmel. Each side would sacrifice an animal to their god, and the god that sent rain to extinguish the fire would be the true God. The winner was the God of Israel! He gave Elijah a great victory. Yet, when Elijah heard that the pagan queen, Jezebel, was out to get him, he reacted in fear and depression and hid in a cave. God demanded to know what Elijah was doing there and suggested that he get up, eat and drink, and listen for God's voice. God did not speak in the wind or the fire or the earthquake, but in the still small voice, a gentle whisper, that gave him direction for his future. In the time of his discouragement, Elijah failed to "see" what God had done in his life (1 Kings 19:10-21).

Though sometimes we fall into pessimism like Elijah, we *can* learn to cultivate a positive outlook—an outlook that sees the truth of the big picture. I think of the elegant and graceful figure skater Michelle Kwan, who saw her situation with clear perspective. She was favored to win the gold medal in the women's figure skating competition at the 1998 Winter Olympics, yet an unexpected brilliant performance by Tara Lipinski gave this newcomer the gold. Following the Olympics, a TV reporter asked Michelle, "How did it feel to lose?" Michelle looked at her in astonishment and said, "I didn't lose. I won the silver." Likewise, when we are fatigued or fearful, we often fail to see what others can see clearly.

Once, on a flight from Orlando, Florida, to Atlanta, Georgia, my seatmate was a young woman doing battle with a determined two-year-old. Remembering that I had in my briefcase a pop-up book for a friend's child named Elana, I sought to distract the blonde, curly-haired little boy. As I began to read the book aloud, he climbed from his mother's lap into mine. By the third reading, he was sound asleep, tightly clutching his new treasure.

The young woman thanked me profusely and then told me how unhappy she was because her husband, a naval lieutenant, was being transferred to Newport News, Virginia. She didn't want to go because she had good friends in Florida who were her support system and babysitters she could count on. She was afraid that she couldn't find either of these in a new place, and she dreaded the loneliness she would experience when her husband was at sea. In fact, she was ready to give up on the marriage. My temptation was to say, "Grow up, kid," but I knew she was hurting. So, instead, I said, "Tell me about your husband."

As she answered, I felt she was speaking more to herself than to me. "He is a great father and a good husband. He is not an alcoholic, or unfaithful, or abusive—sometimes argumentative, but never abusive—and he wants his family with him." It was when she showed me his picture that I knew she really didn't want a divorce.

"It sounds to me as if you are fatigued from the constant care of three children under age six and afraid of losing your support system," I said.

"Right on both counts," she replied.

"May I make a few suggestions?" I asked cautiously.

"Please do," was her quick reply.

Among other things, I suggested that she talk honestly with her husband about her feelings and ask for his help in the transition. Then I suggested that they find a church home immediately upon their move. "It will be good for you, for Bill, and for the children; and it is a great place to make new friends. In the meantime, give thanks every day for a husband who loves you and for healthy, intelligent children."

By this time, the plane had landed, and we were walking into the Hartsfield Airport with Timmy skipping ahead, holding Elana's book, which she never saw. The young woman gave me a hug as we parted and whispered, "Everything looks so different to me now."

Yes, we need to focus on the truth of the big picture,

remembering God's faithfulness and goodness. If we will do this, we will know the truth, "and the truth will set [us] free" (John 8:32 NIV).

You Can Use Your "Eagle Eyes" Eyesight to Inspire and Motivate Others

At the height of the Great Depression, which lasted from 1929 to 1942, President Franklin Delano Roosevelt gave his first inaugural address. On that day, March 4, 1933, he spoke to a financially bankrupt nation. His now famous words, "There is nothing to fear but fear itself," breathed hope into a dispirited people and galvanized them into action. It took a long time for the nation to recover completely, but most historians agree that it was that statement that initiated the recovery.

President Roosevelt saw the big picture. He didn't just focus on one part of the scenario, such as financial disaster; instead, he focused on the whole spectrum. He knew that Americans could never rebuild until they believed in themselves and in their government again. He perceived their needs and their deep desires and responded accordingly.

A similar thing happened during World War II. Adolf Hitler had successfully invaded France, and many military experts felt that the British Isles would be next. They knew that England was ill equipped and ill prepared, and they predicted that the nation would be defeated within weeks. No Allies were coming to England's defense. America was not ready to go to war, and Russia was not then interested in participating.

May we never underestimate our own potential for influence.

The experts were wrong. They had not taken the measure of a sixty-year-old politician named Winston Churchill, who only six months earlier had been named British prime minister. In 1982, when Ralph and I were in England for a ministerial exchange at West Kirby, we were amazed at the number of people who, though many were children at the time, remembered the gravelly voice of the prime minister as he called the nation to arms in his speech to the House of Commons on June 18, 1940. In part, he told them that France had fallen, and that it was certain the enemy would next turn his wrath upon them. He said that Hitler had to take their island if he were to win the war. He also reminded them that England's future and that of the entire Christian civilization would be affected by their actions. Then he said these oft-quoted words: "Let us brace ourselves and so bear ourselves that if Great Britain and the Commonwealth last for a thousand years, men will say, 'This was their finest hour.'"

Franklin Delano Roosevelt and Winston Churchill used their "eagle eyes" eyesight to inspire and motivate others, and they changed the course of history. May we never underestimate our own potential for influence. God is ready and waiting to use us!

You Can Use Your "Eagle Eyes" Eyesight to Share Jesus' Power to Change Lives

The power of Christ to change lives is the same yesterday and today. It is the same power that confronted Saul on the road to Damascus and turned this brilliant murderer, who was on his way to commit more murders, into a dynamic disciple. I never tire of reading this amazing story (Acts 9:1-19). Saul saw a light from heaven shining so brightly that he fell to the ground. Then he heard a voice, asking

"Saul, Saul, why do you persecute me?"
"Who are you, Lord?" Saul asked.

"I am Jesus, whom you are persecuting," he
replied. "Now get up and go into the city, and you
will be told what you must do." (Acts 9:4-6 NIV)

Saul, who lost his sight in this powerful experience, went into
Damascus as Jesus directed. Meanwhile, the disciple Ananias in
Damascus was directed in a vision to go to the house of Judah on
Straight Street and ask for a man named Saul, whose sight would
be restored when Ananias laid his hands on him and prayed.
Ananias had heard of the terrible things Saul had done to
Christians, so he didn't want to obey the order. In the end, how-
ever, Ananias "turned his eyes upon Jesus" rather than upon Saul's
past. Saul's sight was restored, the conversion was complete, and
the world was forever changed.

Is it possible to see such power at work in our world today?
Through many years of ministry, Ralph and I have seen married
couples reconcile, agnostics become believers, weary disciples be
energized, and grim Christians become joyous. None of these is
more powerful than the experience of Reid.

Ralph was asked by a businessman in our church to call on Reid
after he was diagnosed with leukemia and was expected to have
only three months to live. Reid was an agnostic. As a child, he
had gone regularly with his mother to Sunday school and church.
But when teachers and pastors had not taken seriously the prob-
ing questions of a child's brilliant and inquiring mind, he gave up
Christianity as being superstition, even myth. He had been a
good athlete and an excellent student in high school and college.
He went on to succeed in business, seemingly without even trying. By the time we came to know him, however, his marriage
had failed and his wife had remarried. His teenage son was living
with him and was on drugs. It was not a peaceful life.

Reid greeted Ralph warmly, listened courteously, and promised
to read what Ralph left him, including the Gospels. Ralph spoke

in a straightforward manner about God's love for us and about what God has done for us through Christ. The seed was planted and found root in the fertile soil of Reid's heart.

As Reid's body grew weaker, he was in and out of the finest hospitals in the country. Once, in Chattanooga, he had what can only be described as a vision of Jesus. He told us that his room was so full of love and light that he felt tears running down his cheeks. Jesus stood at the foot of his bed and spoke clearly to Fred, saying that he would be healed. Then with a smile, he added, "Your blood count will go up, and you will go skiing in March." When I heard the story, it sounded a bit "hokey" to me. Surely this had only been a dream. Yet Reid was on the ski slopes in Colorado in March of that year, and now, twenty-five years later, he is one of the strongest Christians and churchmen I have ever known. Reid's son has been drug-free for years and was led to Christ by his father. Reid remarried, and, though doctors said that he likely would never have children because of all the radiation he received, they now have two healthy and handsome children.

> *If we allow the love and grace of Jesus Christ to flow through us to others, our very lives can become a witness to his power.*

Reid is a living testimony that "our God is able" (Daniel 3:17 TLB), yet we must have the spiritual eyes to "see." All around us are people who, like Reid, want to believe their lives can be different. If we allow the love and grace of Jesus Christ to flow through us to others, our very lives can become a witness to his power. And if we are faithful in our love and service to others, we can share, when they are ready, the biblical witness to Christ's power as well as our own faith journey. Then we will become instruments through which Christ's awesome, life-changing power becomes operative in them.

Digging a Little Deeper

1. Read Psalm 139:14. As you consider the facts about the eyesight of eagles (pp. 77-78), what thoughts occur to you? What other creatures or things in our world strike you with the intricate and awesome power of our Creator? What about your own life makes you know that you are "fearfully and wonderfully made"?

2. What do you think enabled Franklin D. Roosevelt and Winston Churchill to see the big picture rather than to stay focused on the disaster of financial depression and the tragedy of war? Think of someone you know personally who has this kind of big picture eyesight. How does this person motivate and inspire others?

3. Do you believe that the ability to grasp the big picture is an attribute we are born with, or do you believe we develop this ability as we grow in faith? Explain your answer.

4. If you had been Michelle Kwan, how might you have reacted to the reporter's question after the Olympics? Is your tendency to bog down in self-pity and withdraw into depression, or to look optimistically for the truth of the big picture? Why? How does faith in Christ help us have hope? How should this hope affect our outlook on our circumstances and our lives?

5. Reread Acts 9:1-19. Have you observed in others or experienced in your own life the transforming power of Christ as evidenced in the conversion of Saul or in the complete healing—body, mind, and spirit—of Reid? How can you share the healing power of Jesus Christ with others?

7

Be Compassionate

"But a certain Samaritan, as he journeyed, came where he was. And when he saw him, he had compassion." (Luke 10:33 NKJV)

"But while he was still far off, his father saw him and was filled with compassion; he ran and put his arms around him and kissed him."

(Luke 15:20 NRSV)

arly in my parenting days, I heard an oft-repeated phrase: "Tell me a story." Years later I heard the same request from my grandchildren. In retrospect, I realize that much of our family history and value system are passed on through stories, for they enter our thoughts and imaginations in a way we can never forget.

Jesus was a master storyteller, and he did much of his teaching through parables, or stories. Two of the ones most remembered are the parables of the good Samaritan (Luke 10:30-37) and the prodigal son (Luke 15:11-32). The good Samaritan teaches us that our neighbor is anyone in need, regardless of race, ethnicity, or status; that we are not to walk on the other side when we see people in need; that compassion is one of the strongest attributes of Christians. Our Lord exemplified this so beautifully while he was here on this earth. Obviously, not everyone has received this message; but for Christians, it is a part of our psyches.

The beloved story of the prodigal son not only tells us of the unconditional love of God, but also paints a picture in living color and intricate detail. George Murray has called the parable of the prodigal son "the most divinely tender and the most humanly touching story ever told on earth" (*Jesus and His Disciples*, p. 163). Likewise, George Buttrick has said, "No story more instantly touches the nerve of actual life" (*The Parables of Jesus*, New York: Baker Book House, 1973, p. 189).

In a city where we once lived, there was a couple we greatly admired. They were intelligent, well-educated, strong Christians who were influential in their church and community. Their only son received from them a strong heritage of faith, a fine education, and unconditional love. Things went well until the son, Bob, went away to college. Before midterm of his freshman year, he telephoned to say that he had dropped out of college and was going to "bum around the country" for a while. Despite their pleas, he was on his way. There would be weeks, even months, of not knowing where he was.

Finally, the day came when the telephone rang and their son asked, "May I please come home?" Despite the painful anguish of that period, the couple received their son lovingly and helped him become established on a different path that led to a college degree and a happy marriage. I thought of them immediately when I heard the compassionate words of Mary Lu Walker's "Runaway Song." She tells of her son who left home, traveled far and wide, and never told her why. Then, one day, when times were hard for him, he asked if she would let him in if he knocked on her door. Her reply was like that of the prodigal son's father. She said: "You could knock upon my door, and I'd run to let you in."

On the campus of a small Christian college in Montreat, North Carolina, there is the most amazing life-size fresco of the parable of the prodigal son. The only disturbing figure in the entire scene is the elder brother, whose face is contorted with jealousy, anger, pride, and judgment. He obviously didn't recognize the soul-destroying power of his sinful attitude. He, too, was a prodigal. Because he refused to sit under the roof with his brother, he denied himself entrance into his father's house.

We can be prodigals whether we are in a far country or in our own backyards. Yet we are the ones who suffer most, for we lose so much when we refuse to be the compassionate people we were created to be. We were created in the image of our God, who "is gracious and compassionate, slow to anger and rich in love" (Psalm 145:8 NIV). Compassion should be a defining characteristic of our lives. In fact, we are made in such a way that we actually function better when compassion is part of our lifestyle.

Eagle People Reach Out to Others in Love

. As strange as it may sound, God made the eagle, a large bird of prey, to be compassionate. I knew before I began my study of eagles that they were competitive. If an eagle spots a fish that would make a good dinner for the family, he will fight to the finish to retrieve it. I didn't know, however, how compassionate they are.

Like humans, eagles sometimes become sick or depressed. When this happens, they fly into a nearby valley to recover or die. Several years ago, I spoke in Phoenix, Arizona, and I mentioned this fact about the eagle. Some participants told me about such a valley in their area called "The Valley of the Crying Eagles." In this and many similar valleys throughout our land, the well eagles regularly fly into the valley to take food and encouragement to the sick eagles and try to get them into the air again. The well eagles don't stay in the valley, but they go there in compassion to help the sick.

This, to me, is a perfect analogy for what the body of Christ should be in the world. After all, the word *compassion* literally means "with heart." Compassion, then, means to reach out to others with the heart. That kind of love is the most powerful in the world.

Some years ago I had the privilege of teaching a large adult Sunday school class. It was a class of great diversity, ranging in ages from early twenties to midsixties. Some were married; some were single. Some were seekers; some had been committed Christians for years. It was an exciting challenge! One Sunday morning, something happened that solidified my belief that the Body of Christ (the church) is to be a caring, sharing, redemptive fellowship.

In the class was a woman named Susan who had gone through an extremely painful and unwanted divorce. She had seemed to walk through it with grace and dignity and had maintained her Sunday school and church attendance. None of us knew the depth of her despair. One Sunday morning I was teaching when Susan walked in uncharacteristically late. She took an aisle seat beside the only vacant seat in the room. Immediately a woman named Betty, who was sitting on the other side of the room, got up from beside her husband and walked quietly and unobtrusively around the back of the room to sit beside Susan—the only person in the room who was sitting alone. It was an intuitively compassionate act, and I made a mental note to thank her after class. After class, however, these two women went across the hall to talk seriously and privately in another classroom.

When I returned home after lunch with Ralph, the telephone was ringing. "Nell, let me tell you what happened," Betty said. She told me that when the class ended, she turned to Susan and said, "The way you have handled this very difficult time has been a Christian witness and an inspiration to us all." Susan burst into tears, and Betty guided her across the hall for privacy. Susan produced a suicide note that she had planned to leave on the car seat beside her when she drove home after church, planning to close the garage door and leave the car engine running.

"If she had planned to do something so drastic, why do you think she came to Sunday school and church today?" I asked Betty. She told me that she had asked Susan that very question, and Susan's reply was this: "Maybe it was a lifetime habit, or maybe it was a desperate cry for help."

> *In Acts 10:38, Luke tells us that Jesus "went about doing good" (NRSV). Here he is speaking of not the great act of salvation, but the small daily acts of kindness.*

Her reply made me realize anew the value of regular attendance in Sunday school and church. I also realized that God had prepared Betty to hear and heed Susan's cry for help. Betty and her husband, along with several other class members, stayed close to and supported Susan through a period of readjustment and recovery. During that time, they encouraged Susan to talk with a Christian counselor, which she did. The happy ending is that Susan not only found healing, but also began to work as a facilitator in a divorce recovery group in our church's singles' ministry. Five years later, she was married to a Christian man whose wife had died three years earlier.

Throughout this episode, I recalled something I had heard Alan McGinnis, a well-known Christian counselor and author, say in a seminar I once attended. He remarked that if churches truly became redemptive fellowships, full of compassion and support, then the suicide rate and the number of people who enter mental institutions would radically drop. Susan's story certainly is a strong affirmation of this. In Acts 10:38, Luke tells us that Jesus "went about doing good" (NRSV). Here he is speaking of not the great act of salvation, but the small daily acts of kindness. As twenty-first-century disciples who are part of the "Body of Christ," we are called upon to do the same.

Eagle People Treat Others with Graciousness

As we reach out to others, we need to remember that compassion is not feeling sorry for others or treating them in a patronizing manner. True compassion is reaching out graciously, always aware of the feelings of others. We are to imitate our Lord, whose graciousness is portrayed throughout the Gospels. The story of the healing of the woman who had been hemorrhaging for twelve years is a wonderful example (Luke 8:40-48).

Jesus was on the way to the home of Jairus, a ruler in the synagogue who asked Jesus to come heal his sick daughter. This was a fortuitous invitation since many of the Pharisees not only were suspicious of Jesus, but also deeply resented him. The disciples were trying to move Jesus quickly through the crowds when the hemorrhaging woman touched the hem of his garment and was healed.

"Who touched me?" Jesus asked.

Peter, rather impatiently, I imagine, chided Jesus, saying, "Master, the people are crowding and pressing against you."

But Jesus said, "Someone touched me; I know that power has gone out from me" (Luke 8:45-46 NIV).

When the woman came forward to tell her story, Jesus knew that her malady caused her to be considered unclean and that

> *In a fragmented, often violent world, we are to be the visible instruments of Christ's love and power. This means serving others with compassion regardless of ethnicity, status, or creed.*

anyone who touched anything she had touched or sat or lain on would be considered unclean (Leviticus 5:19-28). She could not live as a wife with her husband; she could not worship at the synagogue; she could not go to social events. No doubt she was physically weak, emaciated, unable to stand for any period of time, and lonely to the core. Yet Jesus was not patronizing or judgmental or hurried in the least. He gave her the feeling that she was understood, using a term of endearment and respect when he said, "Daughter, your faith has healed you. Go in peace" (Luke 8:48 NIV).

In a fragmented, often violent world, we are to be the visible instruments of Christ's love and power. This means serving others with compassion regardless of ethnicity, status, or creed. Imagine for a moment what a difference Christ can make in our world if we are willing to be his instruments!

Digging a Little Deeper

1. Reread the story of Susan (pp. 90-91). Why do you think she went to Sunday school and church that Sunday morning? Why was Betty's quiet and unobtrusive move so significant to Susan? What message do you think it communicated to her?

2. Have you ever felt that you were at the end of your rope? How would you describe that time in your life? Who (or what)

helped you? If an individual or individuals reached out to you, whether consciously or unconsciously, how were they acting on the apostle Paul's words found in Galatians 6:2? In what way were they fulfilling the law of Christ?

3. Read the parable of the good Samaritan (Luke 10:25-37). Why do you think the priest and Levite passed by on the other side? In what ways do we do this today? Why do you think this is so? Describe a contemporary "good Samaritan" you have heard about or know personally.

4. Read the parable of the prodigal son (Luke 15:11-32). Which character do you most identify with—the father, the prodigal son, or the elder son? Why?

5. Even children from strong Christian homes go through periods of rebellion. Because circumstances can be so different, there is not one "right way" to handle a child's rebellion. Would you agree, however, that compassion should always play a role, even when "tough love" is necessary? Why or why not? And if so, how?

6. In what way(s) is the compassion of the well eagles in the valley (pp. 89-90) an analogy for us—as individuals and as the church?

7. Read Luke 8:40-48. How can you detect the graciousness of Jesus in this story?

8. Like the woman with the issue of blood, do you need the touch of Christ to make you whole? Where? Why? Write down your feelings of fragmentation and where you need wholeness, and share with a partner or group as you feel comfortable.

9. Respond to this statement: Though we don't know what our future holds, we can know the One who holds the future. Consider/discuss the ways in which you need to grow in faith

(for example, Bible study, prayer, regular worship, regular quiet times with God, small-group study, service, and so forth). Decide when and how you will begin.

An Eagle Challenge

Remember that compassion *means "with heart"—reaching out to others with the power of active love. This is not only thinking about a person, but also connecting with the person in some visible way—such as giving a smile or a word of encouragement, listening with understanding, and helping in tangible ways.*

Who needs your active love today? Will you, in the name of Christ, give that love?

8

Discover the Art of Renewal

"Praise the Lord, . . . who satisfies your desires with good things so that your youth is renewed like the eagle's." (Psalm 103:1a, 5 NIV)

It was a delightfully pleasant morning in Little Cottonwood Canyon. Leaves on the aspen tress were fluttering in the breeze like wind chimes. Being at Snowbird in late July was like being in another world. Sitting on the balcony of our friends' condominium, located at eight thousand feet and looking straight ahead to ski slopes that reach eleven thousand feet, reminded me of the vastness of the universe and the greatness of our God.

In the face of such majesty, it was impossible to think fearful, anxious, or petty thoughts. In fact, I felt a deep, pervasive peace that seemed to permeate every cell of my body. My worries fell away like flies on sticky paper. What a contrast to my reactions when I had arrived at Snowbird two days earlier.

I had been stressed out from too many deadlines arriving at once; writing assignments, speech preparations and presentations, and out-of-town houseguests had combined to put my system on overload. The result was fatigue and overreaction, irritation, anxiety, and a feeling of dis-ease.

When my body and spirit got back in sync, I realized how easily the pressures of our everyday world and our own bad choices put us into a self-destruct pattern. *Eustress,* or good stress that motivates us to peak performance, can quickly become *distress,* causing burnout or, at the very least, a "brownout" that has us living and working at half capacity. In such a state, creativity and joy quickly disappear, causing entropy of the spirit.

Eagle People Recognize Their Need for Regular Renewal

In physics, the law of entropy says that every system left unattended will run down unless it is regularly renewed. This is true of machines, businesses, political systems, churches, civic organizations, marriages, friendships, and the human body, mind, and spirit.

When our children were small, Ralph often had church meetings in the evening, and I sometimes had to be in the house for twenty-four hours a day when one or both children were ill (which seemed constant when they were in preschool). Under stress, even the best marriages experience some form of entropy. Ralph wisely suggested that the two of us get out of the house for a "date night" every two weeks. Whatever happened at home, I knew that I would be able to get out in a few more days. You can stand anything for two weeks!

If we're not careful to guard against it, life can become monotonous, routine, and joyless; and our spirits can become dry, parched, and withered. We must recognize our need for regular renewal, and, like the eagle, we must actively seek it.

Those evenings put fun back into our relationship. It gave us time to talk and allow our inner worlds to touch. In retrospect, I realize what a magnificent gift that was, especially coming from a busy pastor. In fact, at the beginning of each year, he gave me a calendar on which date nights were scheduled for every month. In his own calendar, he circled each of these nights and penciled in "Date with Nellie." When someone asked him to speak on those dates or wanted to schedule a meeting for those times, he could honestly say, "I have a previous engagement." There were a few times when emergencies at the church meant that we had to cancel a date, but they were rare. I always felt that Ralph scheduled prime time, not left-over time, for me. That did wonders for our relationship.

If we're not careful to guard against it, life can become monotonous, routine, and joyless; and our spirits can become dry, parched, and withered. We must recognize our need for regular renewal, and, like the eagle, we must actively seek it.

For years, I have heard a story about eagle renewal that must have come from Native American folklore. The story tells that eagles, when they are old—when their eyes are dim, their beaks are no longer sharp, and their feathers have lost luster—go to a place where there are large rocks. Here they beat themselves until their feathers fall out and their beaks are softened. Then they wait until new, shiny feathers come onto their wings before returning to the family nest—once they have renewed their youth.

Another story of renewal has been meaningful for Christians around the world. According to this legend, when an old eagle's wings become heavy and his eyes become darkened with a mist, he goes in search of a fountain. Then, from over against it, he flies to the height of heaven, even into the circle of the sun. There he singes his wings and, at the same time, evaporates the fog of his eyes in the rays of the sun. At length, he takes a header down into the fountain, dipping himself three times in it. Instantly, he is renewed with great plumage and splendor of vision (listed by Stephen Friar in *Dictionary of Heraldry* [New York: Harmony Books, 1987], quoting the translation of T. H. White).

Earlier Christians around the world, and especially in Europe, adopted the symbolism of this legend. They compared the eagle looking into the sun to Christians looking at the "Son," and the renewal of the eagle's youth through its plunge into the fountain to the renewal of the soul through baptism. Even today, an eagle may be seen on the baptismal fonts in some older churches.

Like the eagle, we don't have to be worn down by life. We don't have to live in burnout. We don't have to live devoid of creativity and joy. The solution is spiritual renewal through Jesus Christ, the "bread of life" and "living water." Christ is ready to renew old and tired spirits, if we will allow it. Let's consider some of the practical ways we can seek renewal through Christ.

Six Steps to Renewal Through Christ

Obviously, we can't always remove ourselves from a stressful situation to a place of beauty and peace, though we should try to do this at least once a year. There are some simple steps, however, that we can always take to counteract entropy and renew our spirits through Christ.

1. Daily cultivate a calm center in your inner spirit

Each time I read of a tornado or cyclone wreaking havoc on homes and cities and people's lives, I remember the words of Edwin Markham: "At the heart of the cyclone tearing the sky is an eye of central calm" (in "A Place of Peace" printed in *1,000 Quotable Poems,* New York: Harper and Brothers, 1937). Our lives at work and at home may require fast-paced, even hectic movement, yet, in our "central control," we can be calm and peaceful. Despite the fact that we cannot always control what happens to us or around us, we *can* control what happens within us!

Acknowledging that God has given us a will and the ability to control our thoughts and our responses is the first step toward cultivating a calm center within. Just as creating a time and place for quietness is an act of the will, so also we must allow Christ, who lives within us, to give us his peace.

2. *"Set your sails" for the day*

Most people have more they need to do or want to do than they have hours in the day. So "setting your sails" for the day must be a conscious priority. In fact, there is no way to achieve a calm center in your inner spirit without the planned neglect of something else.

In my own life, I have observed an early morning "quiet time" for meditating on scripture, praying, and planning my day since I was in college. It was then that I also began the practice of journaling. If ever I want to see God's direction in my life, I simply go back and read my journals over the years. (Try it, and you, too, will be amazed by what God has done!) For me, early morning has worked well for this discipline because it is a time before interruptions begin—a telephone needing to be answered, children clamoring for attention, or simply a chore needing to be done. Although this habit has meant the neglect of sleep time, which has not been easy for this sleepyhead, it has always been beneficial.

> *You must seek [God] in the morning, if you want him through the day!*
> *—Ralph Cushman, "My Secret"*

Thousands of years ago, the psalmist and the prophet Isaiah indicated that God speaks to and renews his creation: "Be still, and know that I am God!" (Psalm 46:10 NRSV); "Praise the Lord, . . .

who satisfies your desires with good things so that your youth is renewed like the eagle's" (Psalm 103:1a, 5 NIV); "But those who hope in the LORD will renew their strength. They will soar on wings like eagles; they will run and not grow weary, they will walk and not be faint" (Isaiah 40:31 NIV). Likewise, in John 10:10, Jesus reminds us: "I have come that they might have life, and have it to the full" (NIV). Taking time early in the morning to think, meditate, and pray to our eternal God provides resources that are unavailable if we get up in a hurry and rush pell-mell through our days.

The late Methodist Bishop Ralph Cushman wrote a wonderful poem entitled "My Secret." His closing lines ring so true: "So I think I know the secret. . . . You must seek [God] in the morning if you want him through the day!" (*Spiritual Hilltops,* Nashville: Abingdon Press, 1932).

3. *Plan and organize your time*

It sounds obvious, yet so often we simply neglect to do it. The truth is, much of our distress comes from drifting. Instead of organizing our lives around a central purpose, setting goals, and following through, we procrastinate, vacillate in indecision, and waste time. Time management is easy to write about but difficult to manage. For years, despite my best intentions, I seemed to have too many tasks left over at the end of each twenty-four-hour day. There were times when I wanted to throw in the towel and say, "I'll never do this. My life is out of control." What I have learned through the years is that no one time-management plan works for everyone. It is easy to become a "time nut." I discovered that I wasn't as interested in becoming efficient as becoming an authentically effective Christian.

The following three steps have simplified the process for me:

- Stay close to Christ.

- Set four to six "ultimate goals"—what you want your life eventually to become or achieve. (More about this in step 4.)
- Each evening, write down the six most important things you want to accomplish the following day. This helps you get a running start on the next time period.

Amazingly, this last discipline has allowed me to become more spontaneous. For example, it has allowed me to drop everything and go on a family picnic when everyone else's schedule permitted, or to sleep late after a series of unusual stresses or deadlines—without feeling guilty!

Jesus reminded the Pharisees, "The Sabbath was made for man, not man for the Sabbath" (Mark 2:27 NIV). Likewise, every day is a gift from God, and I believe that if Jesus were to talk to us today about time management, he might say, "Time is not for filling twenty-four-hour segments, but for developing balanced spiritual wholeness in my people." This leads us to our next "step" to renewal.

4. Stay balanced

The secret to simplifying your life is to stay balanced. A successful career woman told me that, sadly, she had taken little time for anything except work. As a result, her marriage was in shambles, she dropped her friends one by one, her spirits were dry and withered, and she no longer felt joy in living. All of that could have been avoided if she had strived for balance in her life. Prayerfully setting ultimate goals is one of the best ways to ensure we maintain balance.

> **As Christians, our ultimate goals are not just what we want them to be, but what we believe God wants them to be.**

It was ten years ago that I heard Peter Drucker, the business guru, say, "Before you set any short-term business or personal goals, set your ultimate goals. Determine where you want to be when you come to retirement or to the end of your life." That was a new idea to me. Of course, as Christians, our ultimate goals are not just what we want them to be, but what we believe God wants them to be—which we determine by seeking God's direction through silence, prayer, and meditation on God's Word.

I have only slightly altered the four ultimate goals I wrote down that day: to live authentically under the value system I have chosen, the Christian faith; to be able to give and receive love, especially to the significant others in my life; to make a contribution of real worth through using the two talents I have discovered—speaking and writing—and to go to heaven when I die. As Peter Drucker explained, our short- and long-term goals in every facet of life should be moving us toward our ultimate goals. When all our goals are God-centered and connected in this way, we find a sense of balance and fulfillment in our daily living, despite the ups and downs of everyday life.

Joe and Karen Clumpner have this sense of balance and fulfillment. They are our delightful next-door neighbors who are both loving parents and adventurous grandparents. They are well educated, widely traveled, and strongly committed Christians. In fact, they met in a navigator's program for students at Harvard. They both have been teachers—he at a church-related college and she at a private girls' school. Two years ago, just before Joe's so-called retirement, they took a group of his students to study in China for a semester. The Chinese were so impressed with the credentials of the Clumpners that the government invited them to return to China as university professors. Since then they have spent nine months each year living in a Communist country under conditions that are spartan because they have some ultimate goals, one of which is to lead others, especially young people, to faith in Jesus Christ. The results have been amazing. I call them spiritual Marco Polos who travel lightly except for a huge supply of faith in an awesome God. Herein is the secret of living a balanced life.

5. Take care of your health

This one is so obvious that it almost seems unnecessary to mention, yet so many of us neglect our health. Our health is a priceless gift, which, if lost, can cause us to give up our dreams or, at least, to put our lives on hold.

In his book *Titan: The Life of John D. Rockefeller, Sr.* (New York: Random House, 1998, p. 332), Ron Chernow tells a fascinating story about the Titan who, at his death, was the world's richest man. Reared in very humble circumstances, Rockefeller worked hard and worried himself into ulcers on his climb up the ladder to CEO of Standard Oil, the largest oil monopoly of its time. Some of his stresses came from hundreds of charitable organizations beseeching him for money. By the time he was fifty, he had such bad digestive problems that his complete diet consisted of crackers and milk. He didn't expect to live until the end of the decade. Then, one day, he read an article entitled "Try Giving Yourself Away," which suggested that we should give not only our money, but also our smiles, our encouragement, our kindness, and our service to others in gratitude for what we have been given. Slowly but surely, Rockefeller began to learn the joy of giving. He also began to eat nutritionally and to enjoy people—and life itself—and he lived to be ninety-eight.

Consider how much stress and illness we could alleviate from our lives simply by eating nutritionally, exercising regularly, getting adequate sleep, avoiding needless worrying, living within our incomes, and giving generously. Common sense is an important step to both physical and spiritual renewal! In a fast-paced world in which the multitudinous activities and demands can suck the very life out of us, we can choose to take care of ourselves and live in power. In addition to caring for our physical bodies, we can claim our Christian heritage and God-given strengths, choose positive emotions, and affirm words of promise and encouragement from the Bible, such as, "The Lord is the strength of my life" (Psalm 27:1 NKJV) and "The joy of the LORD is [my] strength" (Nehemiah 8:10 NKJV). Although being positive by conditioning our minds with biblical affirmations may not make us physically strong or healthy, it will give us spiritual power to become all that we were created to be. And this leads us to the next and final step to renewal.

6. Live with positive hope and joy

If we want to counteract entropy and renew our spirits, we must be positive instead of negative. As we discussed in chapter 5, negativism has become a habitual thought pattern for many people, yet we *can* interrupt the pattern. We can learn to look for the best in others instead of focusing on their faults and complaining when they do not measure up to our expectations. We can learn to look for the good in circumstances, as well, as we discussed in detail in chapters 4 and 6. And we can learn to transform our attitudes "by the renewing of [our] minds" (Romans 12:2 NRSV), by taking "every thought captive to obey Christ" (2 Corinthians 10:5 NRSV). As we've already seen, biblical affirmations play a vital role in this process, infusing us with spiritual optimism and power.

> *If we want to avoid burnout, we must learn to enjoy and appreciate life, not complain about it. We must learn to count our blessings and "continually offer to God a sacrifice of praise."*
> *(Hebrews 13:15 NIV)*

Negative emotions, distrust, and despair, which are the opposite of hope, only serve to limit our own abilities and dry up our laughter. If we want to avoid burnout, we must learn to enjoy and appreciate life, not complain about it. We must learn to count our blessings and "continually offer to God a sacrifice of praise" (Hebrews 13:15 NIV), remembering that "all things work together for good for those who love God" (Romans 8:28 NRSV). In fact, joy is an automatic by-product of praise. Give it a try and see for yourself!

Do *You* Need Spiritual Renewal?

Sir Henry Stanley was the journalist who wrote of visiting and interviewing David Livingstone in Africa. According to the story, which I have heard in sermons for years, Stanley contracted with a native of Africa, who was also a Livingstone convert to the Christian faith, to be his guide. At Stanley's urging, the two men traveled through the jungle at breakneck speed. On the fourth morning, the guide refused to move. In frustration, Stanley demanded to know why. "I need time for my spirit to catch up with my body," he said. Incidentally, from his contact with the guide and Dr. Livingstone, Henry Stanley moved from skepticism to the Christian faith, from being an agnostic to being a persuasive Christian.

Sometimes our spirits need to catch up with our bodies. We desperately need spiritual renewal. Christ, and Christ alone, can renew our spirits so that our "youth is renewed like the eagle's" (Psalm 103:5 NRSV). As Paul tells us in 2 Corinthians 5:17, "Therefore, if anyone is in Christ, he is a new creation; the old has gone, the new has come!" (NIV). Let's accept this exciting offer for renewal.

An Eagle Challenge

I challenge you to give up old, tired ways and patterns that drain your energy and leave you joyless. Study carefully the six steps suggested in this chapter, and choose at least one of these to begin implementing today. Begin whether you feel like it or not! Also, honestly answer the following questions (in "Digging a Little Deeper"). You can become a new person in Christ. Your spirit will feel buoyant again, and you will soar like an eagle!

Digging a Little Deeper

1. When was the last time you experienced renewal? Where were you when your spirit caught up with your body? Who or what helped you most in this experience? Relive it with yourself or with a group.

2. Read Matthew 11:28. What promise does Jesus make in this verse? Have you experienced the fulfillment of this promise in your own life? If so, how? How much time do you spend in fellowship with Christ daily? How does this affect Christ's ability to renew you?

3. Do you spend much time in frustration, indecision, or aimless drifting? If not, how are you able to avoid them? If so, which of the following time-management steps do you feel you most need to take, and why: determining your life purpose, setting goals,

following through on decisions, giving up procrastination, organizing your time? Choose one, and start today.

4. What are your priorities? Look carefully at how you spend your time and money, and you will know. Read John 10:10. When Jesus speaks of the abundant life he came to bring us, do you think he was speaking of physical or mental or spiritual power—or a combination of all three? Explain your answer. If you are brutally honest, how much balance and power and "abundant life" are evident in your life? What changes, if any, do you need to make?

5. Which of the following do you most need in order to renew your health: exercise, nutritionally sound eating habits, worry-free living (Philippians 4:6-7), adequate rest, debt reduction? What can you do to begin working on this area? What resources might you consult for advice or counsel? Write a plan of action, and begin implementing it today.

6. Do you find it difficult to be optimistic and joyful in the world in which we live? Why or why not? Josephus, an early Jewish historian, is reported to have said that the first-century Christians "outlived [lived better, not longer], out loved, and out laughed all the people around them." In light of all the persecutions they faced, how would you explain their joy? Read 1 Peter 3:15. What does this verse encourage us to do? Are you prepared to give an "answer" if asked? What would that answer be? What can you do to increase your level of hope and joy?

7. Read 1 Thessalonians 5:18. What does this scripture tell us to do? Why do you think this is God's will for us? Follow Paul's suggestion by counting your blessings—either individually or with a group.

9

"God Will Raise You Up on Eagles' Wings"

"You yourselves have seen what I did to Egypt, and how I carried you on eagles' wings and brought you to myself." (Exodus 19:4 NIV)

I looked at the calendar one morning and realized that I was to speak at Siskin Rehabilitation Hospital and School for Handicapped Children. For the past eight years, I had spoken to volunteers at that beautiful facility that brought hope to so many in our city and the surrounding region. I had prepared carefully for the presentation, trying to be sure that I wasn't using even one of the illustrations I had formerly used for this group.

As usual, I arrived a few minutes early to get myself centered before the program began. "It's strange," I thought, "but I don't recognize any of these people from past meetings." Still, I wasn't too concerned, thinking that this was just a new group of recruits. The woman who presented me ended her introduction with these words: "We are so glad to have Nell Mohney as our speaker for all the teachers of preschool children in Hamilton County."

I was stunned! None of the speech I had prepared would be relevant to this group. Evidently, when the call came to speak again at Siskin, I had assumed that it would be to the Siskin Volunteers. I quickly prayed my panic prayer: "Lord, I can't. You can. Please do. Thanks!"

From the time I walked from my seat on the front row to the lectern, the Holy Spirit called to my remembrance a speech I had given years before to preschool teachers in another city. Even the four illustrations I had used were clear as a bell and, fortunately, still relevant. In that small crisis, God had raised me up on eagles' wings! Even now, when I feel I'm in a desperate situation and see no way out, I remember that incident and give thanks. Ours is an awesome God!

Of course, I know that I cannot expect God to put words in my mouth every time I speak unless I do my part. Our minds are a wonderful part of the equipment included in our stewardship. If we cultivate them and use them for God's purposes, and if we allow Christ to live in us through the Holy Spirit, then God can activate the parts of our brain that seem dormant at the moment. On the other hand, if we are mentally lazy or fill our minds with hatred or lust or unhappy thoughts, God has little access. As Proverbs 23:7 tells us, "For as he [or she] thinks in his heart, so is he" (NKJV). And if we will think on the greatness of our God, remembering how he has "raised us up" in times past, we will be strengthened and empowered to meet whatever challenge we may be facing.

God Has Promised to Raise Us Up on Eagles' Wings

The nineteenth chapter of Exodus tells how God gave his covenant to the children of Israel at Mount Sinai. God had delivered them out of Egypt through the dangerous waters of the Red

Sea, and they had received the Ten Commandments. Now, three months later, it was the time to solidify the covenant with the people God was molding into a great nation.

Once again, the children of Israel waited at the foot of Mt. Sinai because it was assumed that God, Yahweh, dwelled there. As Moses waited, the third verse of chapter nineteen says: "The LORD called to him" (NIV). Many great leaders, writers, and artists have tried to explain the mysterious experience of inspiration. It is always the climax to long periods, sometimes even years, of work or fiery experience, deeply felt. Their descriptions of inspiration can be condensed to the words of this third verse: "The Lord called to him."

Before the covenant was given, God reminded the children of Israel that they had been delivered out of Egypt and had experienced the miracle of the parting waters of the Red Sea, which allowed them to cross safely on dry land. "Remember," said God, "how I bore you up on eagles' wings and brought you to myself" (Exodus 19:4 author's paraphrase). Then God promised to be their God; their part was obedience.

> *When we are obedient through faith, God will raise us up on eagles' wings and bring us to himself.*

The old covenant of law was between God and Israel. The new and better way is the covenant of grace—Christ's offer to forgive us our sins and bring us to God through his sacrificial death. (See Hebrews 8:8-12, which is a quotation of Jeremiah 31:31-34, for a comparison of the old and new covenants.) This covenant is new in extent, for it goes beyond Israel and Judah to include all Gentile nations. It also is new in application because it is written on our hearts and in our minds. It offers a new way to forgiveness, not through the animal sacrifice, but through faith in the life, death, and resurrection of Jesus. Yet the requisite for the new covenant is the same as for the old: obedience. In his poem "The Hound of Heaven," Francis Thompson tells us that God is always the initiator, but that we must choose to be obedient if the covenant is to be operative. And when we are obedient through faith, God will raise us up on eagles' wings and bring us to himself. It's a promise, a covenant; and God is faithful to all of his promises (Psalm 145:13).

God Raises Us Up on Eagles' Wings Both in Everyday Crises and in Big Traumas

In the beginning of this chapter, I told of my experience when God helped me through a particular speaking engagement, indicating that God can "raise us up" in the everyday crises of life. So also God can "raise us up" in the big traumas of life, such as the near-drowning experience of Bruce Larson.

Bruce Larson is a big man in every sense of the word. He is big physically—tall and muscular—he is big in his thoughts—his prolific mind has produced twelve books with more than 1.5 million copies in print—he is big in his experience—having served as president of "Faith at Work," visiting fellow at Princeton Theological Seminary, senior pastor of the University Presbyterian Church in Seattle, Washington, and copastor with Dr. Robert Schuller at the Crystal Cathedral in Garden Grove, California. Bruce Larson is also big in influence. Through his books and messages, many people have come to know Christ personally and have matured in their faith.

In the book *Wind and Fire* ([Waco, Tex: Word Publishing, 1984], 21-22), Larson tells of the frightening experience of nearly drowning. He had taken his daughter, Christine, and her friend Maria shelling on a small island in the Gulf of Mexico near their Florida home. As they wandered up and down the beach looking for shells, the wind changed; and a tropical storm slammed against the little island. The three of them ran toward the cove where their boat was anchored. The storm, however, had already pulled the anchor loose, and the boat was drifting out to sea. As he swam toward the boat, he realized that it was moving away faster than he could swim. Then he turned to swim toward the island, but the tide, the wind, and the waves were against him. The rain was coming down in sheets so that he could hardly see.

When he felt fear and panic, he did two sensible things: He took off his sneakers, and he prayed. He said that he thanked God for the incredible adventure of life and expressed how eager he was to see what came next. Then he told about a bizarre thought. He had just invested several thousand dollars in dental bridgework. He complained to God that his wife could have used that money to bury him. Even in the midst of his trauma, he said that he caught himself smiling at the thought.

> *To see God's hand at work in our everyday living is not only a marvelous affirmation of God's power, but also a strong enhancement of our own faith.*

Finally, he relaxed and floated on his back, reasoning that if he could float in a swimming pool, he could stay afloat in the Gulf of Mexico. Over an hour and a half later, he was finally rescued by a tugboat that his resourceful daughter had signaled with her orange shelling bag. Yes, Bruce Larson is a big man, but he is connected to a bigger God who is able to "raise us up on eagles' wings." This belief is expressed so graphically in both the words and music of the chorus "On Eagle's Wings" by Michael Joncas:

> And He will raise you up
> On eagle's wings,
> Bear you on the breath of dawn,
> Make you to shine like the sun,
> And hold you in the palm of his hand.

Do we have eyes to see God's awesome power currently at work in our world? Both Bruce Larson and I saw our rescues as the providence of God rather than the coincidence of fate. To see God's hand at work in our everyday living is not only a marvelous affirmation of God's power, but also a strong enhancement of our own faith.

Trust and Obedience Are Necessary to Access This Mysterious Connection

In speaking of his frightening experience, Bruce Larson wrote: "You must trust God in the storm as well as in the sunlight." It is easy to hear Bruce Larson's injunction to trust God in life's storms, but it is much more difficult to practice it. After all, we are finite human beings who are easily overwhelmed by fear and doubt. First, we must learn to trust in order to become obedient, and then we must be obedient in order to access God's power. There are some practical ways we can do this.

1. Begin to believe and affirm the biblical promises

Though we've discussed biblical affirmations in previous chapters, I cannot overemphasize the importance of conditioning the mind with the promises of scripture. Deuteronomy 33:27 gives one of these promises: "The Eternal God is your refuge, and underneath are the everlasting arms" (NKJV). In chapter 2, I told what happens when the baby eaglet is learning to fly. The mother eagle pushes the baby out of the nest. The father, who has been circling the nest, never taking his eye off his offspring, is ready to dive immediately to pick the eaglet up if he begins to fall.

> *We cannot fall too far or too quickly for God's reach.*

In like fashion, God's eyes are always on us. To paraphrase the old hymn, "His eyes are on the sparrow, and I know He watches me" ("I Sing Because I'm Happy," *The Cokesbury Worship Hymnal,* p. 231). We cannot fall too far or too quickly for God's reach. "Underneath *are* the everlasting arms" (Deuteronomy 33:27 NJKV). This truth is expressed so beautifully in the third stanza of the hymn "The Care the Eagle Gives Her Young" (by R. Deane Postlethwaite, *The United Methodist Hymnal,* Nashville: The United Methodist Publishing House, 1989, p. 118):

> And if we flutter helplessly,
> as fledgling eagles fall,
> beneath us lift God's mighty wings
> to bear us, one and all.

Let us also remember Jesus' promise: "Surely I am with you always, to the very end of the age" (Matthew 28:20 NIV). Affirm these and other biblical promises until they become as much a part of your being as bone and muscle and tissue. In Psalm 119, the psalmist tells us why we should meditate on God's Word: "I have hidden your word in my heart that I might not sin against you. . . . I meditate on your precepts and consider your ways. I delight in your decrees; I will not neglect your word" (vv. 11, 15-16 NIV).

My own experience is that if I make a list of some of these promises and read them regularly, they soon become a part of my memory bank. Then, when difficult situations arise, the appropriate promise comes to mind for guidance and direction. Jesus knew the scriptures so well that when tempted by Satan in the wilderness, he was able to respond to the particular temptation with just the right word (Matthew 4:1-11). When we memorize some of God's promises and meditate on the passages and the context in which they were written, we are affirming God's promises for living. There is no better way to build trust and confidence in God!

2. Hold on to your high moments

God told the children of Israel through Moses that they should remember his presence with them in Egypt and at the Red Sea and be thankful. He knew that along the long road ahead in the wilderness, they would become discouraged and frustrated, and that the only way they could keep faith and hold steady in the difficult days to come would be to remember God's faithfulness.

> *The remembrance of God's presence in the past holds me steady in the present and gives me hope for the future.*

Slowly but surely, I have learned the life lesson that I need to hold onto my high moments—especially when I am discouraged or unsure about the future. The remembrance of God's presence in the past holds me steady in the present and gives me hope for the future.

In 2001, I fell on a freshly mopped hospital floor while visiting a friend. The result was a dislocated shoulder that, while being set, caused nerve damage in my right arm and hand. It took over a year and many therapy sessions to regain what I had lost. Even when the doctor was not very encouraging about the prospects of my regaining full use of my arm, I kept remembering God's strengthening power during the grieving process of the death of our son and my long bout with cancer. Recalling these high moments renewed my faith and set my will to continue therapy. Today, I have full use of my arm and hand—thanks to my orthopedist, my therapist, and, most of all, my faithful God!

3. Take off your "sneakers" and pray!

In the midst of the storm, use Bruce Larson's advice to "take off your sneakers"—in other words, whatever is pulling you down such as fearful thoughts, worries, attachment to "things," destructive habits, rebellion, and so forth—and pray. If we pray, *believing*, our minds are open to receive God's creative thoughts and guidance.

Once while speaking with a singles' group, I used the title "If You Want to Fly, You Have to Get Rid of the Excess Baggage." I knew the group well enough to know that many of them were holding onto old grudges, resentments, and self-pity from former marriages or dating experiences. Unless they could be rid of the things that were pulling them down, they would always be earthbound and unhappy. They were blocking the channels to God's guidance. Only after getting rid of their excess baggage could they open themselves through prayer to God's healing grace, bringing renewed trust.

4. Walk confidently into the future

No matter how often we falter, if with all of our hearts we truly seek him, "God will raise us up on eagles' wings." One of the most fascinating stories to me in the Old Testament is that of Rahab, the prostitute turned believer (Joshua 2; 6:1-25). Despite her unsavory reputation and the fact that she knew little about the God of the Israelites, Rahab, for some strange and unfathomable reason, began to believe in God. In faith and at great risk, she hid two Israelite men who were sent to spy out the city of Jericho, eliciting from them a promise to save her and her family when they destroyed the city. The men kept their promise. Rahab later married one of the spies and became a committed believer; she was even listed in the lineage of our Lord (Matthew 1:5).

> *If we have even a little faith in God, . . . God can transform our lives and enable us to walk confidently into the future.*

From Rahab we learn that if we have even a little faith in God, even "the size of a mustard seed" (Matthew 17:20), God can transform our lives and enable us to walk confidently into the future. And when we are willing to walk obediently and confidently into the future, trusting God, our faith is strengthened all the more, perpetuating a cycle of faith and obedience. Won't you walk confidently into your future? Remember, God promises to "raise you up"!

An Eagle Challenge

When you are at the end of your rope, tie a knot and hang on! Don't lose hope or have tunnel vision. After all, we are not limited by our own resources. God's limitless resources and mighty power are available to us in small trials and in life-threatening traumas. You can count on it!

Review the suggestions in this chapter, and prayerfully consider what you need to do in order to increase your trust and confidence in God.

Digging a Little Deeper

1. Reread the story of my speaking engagement at the Siskin Hospital (pp. 109-10). How do you account for what happened? Have you had a similar experience of being raised up on eagles' wings? Journal about this experience, or share with a partner or group.

2. Read Exodus 19:4. What are the children of Israel supposed to remember? Why do you think this is important as they receive the covenant to be God's people—a holy nation?

3. Read Exodus 19:5. Why do you think God emphasized obedience on their part? Do you think this is important for us today as well? Explain.

4. Reread Bruce Larson's terrifying experience in the Gulf of Mexico (pp. 112-14). What two practical things did he do? Why were these things important? What application can we make for our own lives?

5. Why did it help Bruce Larson to surrender to the water and float rather than fight the waves? How is this analogous to our need to surrender our lives to Christ? Describe a time when you struggled and fought to stay afloat versus a time when you surrendered to Christ and let him keep you afloat.

6. Respond to Bruce Larson's statement: "You must learn to trust God in the storm as well as the sunlight." Why do you think this is so hard? In what ways can the suggestions in this chapter help us trust God in all circumstances? What other ideas do you have for building our faith and trust in God? How do all of these things lead to our obedience?

10

Soar into the Eternal Dimension Through "Nevertheless Faith"

"Because I live, you also will live." (John 14:19 NRSV)

"And whoever lives and believes in me will never die." (John 11:26 NIV)

Nevertheless My lovingkindness I will not utterly take from him, Nor allow My faithfulness to fail. (Psalm 89:33 NKJV)

*A*s I studied and did research on eagles, I was struck by their courage and fearlessness. It is almost as if they intuitively trust the One who created them. We human beings can take a lesson from them. Trusting in our loving Creator is the key to soaring—not only in this life, but also in the life to come.

While on a speaking engagement in Florida, I saw a bumper

sticker that read: "Have a happy forever." That very evening after I finished speaking, an elderly couple came to the front of the church and asked for an appointment to talk.

The next day as we spoke, I looked carefully at the handsome couple. He was a tall, soft-spoken gentleman with a shock of wavy, gray hair. She was in her eighties, as was he, though she walked with the agility of a woman in her fifties. Dressed in a rose linen suit, the lady's slightly lined, smiling face was framed by softly coiffed gray hair. It was she who spoke first.

"This may seem strange to you, because we are people of faith, but we are not sure about life after death. My husband has cancer, and the doctors say that he will not have long to live; so we need reassurance."

Before I could reply, the soft-spoken husband spoke with sudden firmness. He said, "I want to ask a simple question, and I don't want any theological gobbledygook—just a straightforward, unequivocal yes or no."

"That's fair enough," I replied. "Ask your straight question, and I will give you a straight answer."

"If we are Christians, when we die, will we live again? Will we be reunited with each other?"

"The answer is yes."

"How sure are you?"

"Absolutely, positively, one hundred percent sure."

"Why are you so sure?" the handsome man asked with a sense of urgency.

I proceeded to tell him the reasons for my certainty. The Bible clearly teaches life after death for those who love the Lord and have experienced his grace. I quoted passages such as these:

- "Because I live, you will live also." (John 14:19 NKJV)

- "I am the resurrection and the life. He who believes in Me, though he may die, he shall live. And whoever lives and believes in Me shall never die." (John 11:25-26 NKJV)

- "For in the resurrection they neither marry nor are given in marriage, but are like angels in heaven. And as for the resurrection of the dead, have you not read what was said to you by God, 'I am the God of Abraham, the God of Isaac, and the God of Jacob'? He is God not of the dead, but of the living." (Matthew 22:30-32 NRSV)

- "In My Father's house are many dwelling places; if it were not so, I would have told you. I go to prepare a place for you. And if I go and prepare a place for you, I will come again and receive you to Myself; that where I am, there you may be also." (John 14:2-3 NKJV)

- So it is with the resurrection of the dead. What is sown is perishable, what is raised is imperishable. It is sown in dishonor, it is raised in glory. It is sown in weakness, it is raised in power. It is sown a physical body, it is raised a spiritual body. (1 Corinthians 15:42-44*a* NRSV)

I also reminded him that Jesus had appeared to many after his resurrection and that the Resurrection itself was impeccable proof.

Then I remembered a speech I heard Norman Vincent Peale give (Memorial Auditorium, Chattanooga, Tennessee, 1974) in which he shared two parables originally told by Cecil B. DeMille, one of the most famous motion picture directors in Hollywood history who was known for making such grand-scale motion picture epics as *The Ten Commandments*. The first parable concerns a baby in a prenatal state, tucked up under his mother's loving heart.

"Suppose," I said, "that someone came to this unborn baby and said, 'You cannot stay here very long. In a few months you will be born, or you will die out of this present stage.' The baby might stubbornly remonstrate, 'I don't want to leave here. I am comfortable; I am well cared for; I am warm, loved, and happy; I don't want to leave this place.'

"But in the normal course of events, he is born. He does die out of his mother's womb, but what does he find? He feels beneath him strong, loving arms. He looks up into a face tender with love—the face of his mother. He is welcomed, cuddled, and cared for. He might say, 'How foolish I was. This is a wonderful place to which I have come.'

"Then the child grows into manhood, marries, rears his own children, enjoys middle age, and becomes an old man. One day a doctor may say to him, 'You cannot stay here. You are going to die or be born out of this place into another.' The man might remonstrate, 'But I don't want to die. It is warm and pleasant here, and I have my loved ones.'

"But there comes a time when the man does die. What happens then? Is God's nature going to change? Can we not assume that the man will once again feel loving arms beneath him and once again look up into a strong, beautiful face, more lovely than the first face he saw so long ago? Won't he soon be exclaiming, 'This new life is wonderful! I want to remain here forever!'"

The second story was about an experience DeMille had in a canoe on a lake deep in the Maine woods one summer day. He was working on a script, so he let the canoe drift idly. Suddenly, he discovered that he was in shallow water. He could plainly see on the bottom of the lake a large number of water beetles. One of them crawled out of the water and sank his talons in the hull of the boat, and there he died. Three hours later, still floating in the hot sun, DeMille observed an amazing miracle. He noted that the shell of the water beetle was cracking open. A moist head emerged, followed by wings, and finally the winged creature left the dead body and flew into the air. He went farther in half a second than the water beetle could have crawled all day. The dragonfly flew above the surface of the water, but the water beetles below could not see it.

When I finished telling this story, I turned to the handsome elderly couple and asked, "Do you think the Almighty God would do this for a water beetle and wouldn't do it for human beings—the highest of his creations?" I asked.

Smiling, the couple nodded their heads in understanding. "It's what we have believed in our minds, and now we believe it in our hearts," said the terminally ill man.

"Yes," replied the lady, "now we are ready to celebrate Easter."

I always think of these words whenever I think of death. As Christians, we can have confidence in eternal life!

We Can Face Tomorrow If We Confidently Face the Eternal Tomorrow Beyond Death

For a number of years, I had a magnificent obsession to know the truth about life after death. Actually, the desire was born during my college years. When you are young, you have the feeling that death is something that happens only to old people. The possibility of it happening to your peers or to the people closest to you seems so remote that it rarely enters your mind. Yet, during my four years of college, I lost two friends who were classmates, a boyfriend, and a favorite aunt with whom I spent my summer vacations. Their deaths came so quickly that I began to be afraid of loving people lest I experience the pain of losing them.

In late-night dormitory discussions on death, I expressed my belief in life after death because of Jesus' resurrection and his promise that "whoever . . . believes in Me shall never die" (John 11:26 NKJV). Some of my scientific-minded classmates challenged me. "We don't agree with you," they said. "We think that is a myth. It cannot be supported by science." In retrospect, I realize that I shouldn't have been defensive. Even though I couldn't prove eternal life—for eternal things such as love and beauty can never be proved—neither could they disprove it. Yet I am grateful for their challenge because it became the impetus for my searching for honest answers.

I learned many things from the field of science, including the discovery of three strong reasons for believing in eternal life. First, I learned that our bodies are made of earthly elements that can be chemically analyzed. There is a mysterious force that moves the body. This force is called life, but no one knows precisely the seat of its action. It seems to be in the brain, because when you get a clot in the brain tissue, it paralyzes thought and action. Yet, even though this may be the seat of life, it is not the source of it. During the past three decades, more and more biologists have said that the function of the brain is transmissive, rather than productive. To me, this means that God is the Source of the mysterious force called "life." The brain, then, transmits this force to the body.

The second thing I learned from science is that all the cells in our bodies are completely reborn every seven years. I keep hoping that I will get a better-looking body the next time around! Yet the bodily changes don't affect the personality. A person's individuality continues. Our bodies really are an "earthly tent," as the apostle Paul writes in 2 Corinthians:

> For we know that if the earthly tent we live in is destroyed, we have a building from God, a house not made with hands, eternal in the heavens. For in this tent we groan, longing to be clothed with our heavenly dwelling—if indeed, when we have taken it off we will not be found naked. For while we are still in this tent, we groan under our burden, because we wish not to be unclothed but to be further clothed, so that what is mortal may be swallowed up by life. He who has prepared us for this very thing is God, who has given us the Spirit as a guarantee. (5:1-5 NRSV)

One day, my friend and her four-year-old daughter passed a cemetery. The little girl asked, "What is that?" Her mother replied, "We all live in body houses. Sometimes the body gets old or hurt and it has to be placed in the cemetery, but the real person goes on living in a different place. If I pinch you, it hurts your body house, but it doesn't hurt you inside. If I hurt your feelings or make you sad, it hurts you inside, but it doesn't hurt your body house."

Some time later, I was visiting in their home, and the child came in crying because she had fallen. "Are you hurt?" asked her mother. Between sobs, the child replied, "I'm not hurt, but my body house is."

On this earth we do live in body houses, and it is important to take care of these houses because, as Paul says, they are the "temples of God" (1 Corinthians 3:16-17). The real you—the one who will live forever—is your spirit, which lives within the body house. In 1 Corinthians 15:44, Paul reminds us that in death the physical body dies, but it is raised a spiritual body. In our earthly life, then, our greatest care and growth should be in our spirits.

> *Eternal life is not length of days, but quality of life.*

The third lesson I learned from science is that this is an orderly, law-abiding universe. It seems logical, then, that the Creator, who put a migratory instinct in birds to guide them through the trackless sky, will not disregard our own migratory desire to live forever. Jesus himself affirms this conclusion in many verses of the New Testament. Though he does not use the word *immortality*, he does speak seventy times of *eternal life*, explaining that it begins here and now with our belief in him and continues in life after death. What he suggests, then, is that eternal life is not length of days, but quality of life.

In the intervening years since college, I've lost both of my parents, Ralph's parents, a son, and numerous friends. With each death, I have had the constant inner awareness that "whoever lives and believes in Me [Jesus] shall never die" (John 11:26 NKJV). It is this confidence that enables me to face every tomorrow, remembering there is an eternal tomorrow beyond death. In the words of the beautiful hymn by Bill and Gloria Gaither, "Because he lives, I can face tomorrow"!

We Can Conquer Fear with "Nevertheless Faith"

Recently, a friend who is in her fifties telephoned to tell me that she has been diagnosed with stage-four lung cancer. Already it has spread to the liver and lymph nodes. "Nell," she said, "I believe strongly in life after death and feel confident that I will go to heaven. It's the painful experience of dying that frightens me. Can we talk?"

As I write this, I plan to meet with her when she returns from a large medical center where the oncology protocol to be followed will be decided. My mind has returned again and again to my own diagnosis of cancer twelve years ago and the night when fear overwhelmed me. It was the last weekend in February 1991, when Ralph and I were conducting a consultation in a vitally alive church in Tennessee. Following our meetings on Friday and Saturday with various groups and individuals, I was scheduled to speak at a church-wide dinner on Saturday evening, and Ralph was to preach on Sunday morning.

As I dressed to go to dinner, I felt something large and hard in my abdomen. "My new exercise regimen must be working," I thought. "Those abs are really hard, but I wonder why I am not losing weight." For several months I had noticed that my clothes were getting tight over the abdomen. Yet there had been no change in my diet or my calisthenic exercise program. *Is this what is meant by the "middle-age spread"?* I had wondered. It was at that point that I had drastically increased my exercise for "ab flab." *Maybe I have overdone it,* I concluded.

At that point, an ovarian tumor had never entered my mind. I didn't even mention my discovery to Ralph. At about 2:00 A.M., however, I awakened in the clutches of fear. The "what-ifs" were coming fast and furiously to my mind: *What if this is not a hardened muscle? What if it is a tumor? What if it is malignant? What if I die?* I slipped out of bed and prayed earnestly and quietly for two hours.

> *Often it is in our extremities that God has the best opportunities.*

During that time, God brought to my remembrance a book entitled *The Nevertheless Principle,* by Marion Bond West (Old Tappan, N.J.: Chosen Books, 1986). She had written the manuscript when her forty-seven-year-old husband was awaiting surgery for a brain tumor, and she was overcome with "what-ifs." It was her discovery of a "nevertheless faith" that enabled her to deal with the untimely death of her husband of twenty-five years. The entire book was very helpful to me, but the picture that never left my mind during two surgeries and long months of chemotherapy was a fear-faith circle that she used in the introduction to the book. On one side of the circle were her interpretations of the stages of faith: simple faith (belief in Christ, resulting in good thoughts); positive faith (concern for others); active faith (doing for others); abiding faith (deep trust); and, the highest, "nevertheless living" (whatever happens, I trust God for the future). On the other side of the circle were the stages of fear: what-if (doubt and negativism); physical symptoms of terror (dry mouth, sweaty palms); depression (being sad, even morbid; not engaged with life and people); withdrawal (isolation); and hopelessness (suicidal thoughts). Amazingly, in the circle, hopelessness is the closest to "nevertheless faith"—only one step away.

Often it is in our extremities that God has the best opportunities. In my own battle against fear, I had to plant my faith roots much more deeply. I had to go from active faith to abiding faith—deep trust. Like a swimmer who has to let go and trust the water, I had to let go and trust God's Word and the power of Christ not only to save, but also to deliver me from debilitating fear. Gradually, a sense of peace pervaded my being. I didn't know what my future held, but I knew without a shadow of a doubt who held my future!

> *["Nevertheless faith"] requires total surrender of will, but its benefits are unbelievable.*

Three scripture passages were the vehicles by which I moved from apprehension to faith.

- Nevertheless My lovingkindness I will not utterly take from him, Nor allow my faithfulness to fail. (Psalm 89:33 NKJV)
- For God has not given us a spirit of fear, but of power and of love and of a sound mind. (2 Timothy 1:7 NKJV)
- "And behold, I am with you always, even to the end of the age." (Matthew 28:20 NKJV)

Though in the beginning I moved several times each day back and forth from fear to faith, I began to allow these scriptures to penetrate my mind and my spirit. Each day as I grew in my ability to trust, I felt a strange buoyancy of spirit until, one day, I could say and mean, "Nevertheless (whatever happens), I belong to you, O Christ." The words of Paul in Romans 14:8 resonated with me: "If we live, we live to the Lord; and if we die, we die to the Lord. Therefore, whether we live or die, we are the Lord's"

(NKJV). "Nevertheless faith" is a different world. It requires total surrender of will, but its benefits are unbelievable—perceptions clear, relationships strengthen, and even challenges appear doable.

During these past twelve years, I haven't always lived in "nevertheless faith." Especially when I am tired, ill, or face a new difficult situation, I often revert back to my old patterns of fear. Still, I have lived in the "nevertheless dimension," so I know how to return to it. I never want to embrace confusion and clutter again. Perhaps this is what Jesus meant when he said, "Then you will know the truth, and the truth will set you free" (John 8:32 NIV). It is Christ who sets us free from worry and fear, enabling us to live abundantly here and now and forever.

A Final Word

As long as you are on planet Earth, God will care for you as an eagle cares for the eaglet. Both the father and the mother eagle provide the finest care for their baby eaglet. The mother provides a soft nest and food upon request. And when the mother pushes the eaglet out of the nest in order to teach it to fly, the father eagle flies overhead, waiting to rescue his offspring. Likewise, God provides so many blessings throughout our lives—family members who provide for, support, and care for us; friends who enrich our lives; a church family who points us in the right direction; and, most of all, a Savior who forgives our sins and presents us faultless before the throne of God.

So, if you have chosen the path of forgiveness and redemption through Christ, at death, God literally will "raise you up on eagles' wings"! In that glorious moment, perhaps you will hear God say the same words that Neil Armstrong said in 1969 when his space module touched down on the moon: "The Eagle has landed." I don't know about you, but that makes me want to sing the "Hallelujah!" chorus. What a future we have!

Digging a Little Deeper

1. Read John 11:25 aloud. What does Jesus tell Martha about eternal life in this statement? Do you believe this?

2. Respond to this statement: Our earthly journey is mostly a spiritual journey in which we are being prepared for a higher dimension of life. In what ways have you faced your own earthly mortality?

3. Are you afraid of dying? If so, is it the physical experience and pain that may be involved that frighten you? Or, are you unsure of your salvation? Even John Wesley, who had grown up in a minister's family and was himself pious and devoted to service, still lacked that assurance. He received it in his Aldersgate experience on May 28, 1738, when he felt "his heart strangely warmed." If you don't have this assurance, seek it today in a new surrender to Jesus Christ.

4. Jesus didn't talk about the temperature of hell or the furniture of heaven. What did he say about eternal life? Review the Gospels to find his words on the subject. Now read John 14:1-3. What does Jesus promise in these verses? How does this make you feel? Have you allowed this promise of Jesus to become a strong conviction in your life? If not, why?

5. What has been the biggest challenge you have faced during your earthly journey so far? What has helped you most in facing this challenge?

6. Review the "circle of faith" presented on page 128. Which stage best describes where you are right now? What do you think would be required for you to reach the next level? If you are already at "nevertheless faith," what brought you there?

7. I believe three things are required for reaching and remaining in the two highest levels in the "circle of faith" (abiding trust and

"nevertheless faith"): (1) studying God's word, (2) maintaining a daily relationship with Christ through prayer and service, and (3) "letting go" or surrendering your will. Do you need to give any of these requirements more of your attention? What can you do to plant your spiritual roots more deeply? How can you begin today?